PRESIDENT'S MALARIA INITIATIVE

Mali

Malaria Operational Plan FY 2016

Table of Contents

ABBREVIATIONS and ACRONYMS

ACT	Artemisinin-based combination therapy
AL	Artemether-lumefantrine
ANC	Antenatal care
ASC	*Agent de Santé Communautaire* (Community Health Agent)
BCC	Behavior change communication
CDC	Centers for Disease Control and Prevention
CRS	Catholic Relief Services
CSCOM	*Centre de Santé Communautaire* (Community Health Center)
CSREF	*Centre de Santé de Référence* (Referral Health Center)
DHIS 2	District Health Information System 2
DHS	Demographic and Health Survey
EUV	End-use verification survey
EVD	Ebola Virus Disease
FY	Fiscal year
FANC	Focused antenatal care
FELTP	Field Epidemiology and Laboratory Training Program
GHI	Global Health Initiative
Global Fund	Global Fund to Fight AIDS, Tuberculosis and Malaria
GoM	Government of Mali
iCCM	Integrated Community Case Management
IEC	Information, education, communication
IPTp	Intermittent preventive treatment for pregnant women
IRS	Indoor residual spraying
ITN	Insecticide-treated mosquito net
LBMA	*Laboratoire de Biologie Moléculaire Appliquée* (Laboratory of Applied Molecular Biology)
M&E	Monitoring and evaluation
MIP	Malaria in pregnancy
MIS	Malaria indicator survey
MoH	Ministry of Health
MOP	Malaria Operational Plan
MQM	Medicines Quality Monitoring
NMCP	National Malaria Control Program
PMI	President's Malaria Initiative
QA/QC	Quality Assurance/Quality Control
RDT	Rapid diagnostic test
SLIS	*Système Local d'Information Sanitaire* (Health Information System)
SMC	Seasonal Malaria Chemoprophylaxis
SP	Sulfadoxine-pyrimethamine
UNICEF	United Nations Children's Fund
USAID	United States Agency for International Development
USG	United States Government
WHO	World Health Organization

I. EXECUTIVE SUMMARY

When it was launched in 2005, the goal of the President's Malaria Initiative (PMI) was to reduce malaria-related mortality by 50% across 15 high-burden countries in sub-Saharan Africa through a rapid scale-up of four proven and highly effective malaria prevention and treatment measures: insecticide-treated mosquito nets (ITNs); indoor residual spraying (IRS); accurate diagnosis and prompt treatment with artemisinin-based combination therapies (ACTs); and intermittent preventive treatment of pregnant women (IPTp). With the passage of the Tom Lantos and Henry J. Hyde Global Leadership against HIV/AIDS, Tuberculosis, and Malaria Act in 2008, PMI developed a U.S. Government Malaria Strategy for 2009–2014. This strategy included a long-term vision for malaria control in which sustained high coverage with malaria prevention and treatment interventions would progressively lead to malaria-free zones in Africa, with the ultimate goal of worldwide malaria eradication by 2040-2050. Consistent with this strategy and the increase in annual appropriations supporting PMI, four new sub-Saharan African countries and one regional program in the Greater Mekong Subregion of Southeast Asia were added in 2011. The contributions of PMI, together with those of other partners, have led to dramatic improvements in the coverage of malaria control interventions in PMI-supported countries, and all 15 original countries have documented substantial declines in all-cause mortality rates among children less than five years of age.

In 2015, PMI launched the next six-year strategy, setting forth a bold and ambitious goal and objectives. The PMI Strategy for 2015-2020 takes into account the progress over the past decade and the new challenges that have arisen. Malaria prevention and control remains a major U.S. foreign assistance objective and PMI's Strategy fully aligns with the U.S. Government's vision of ending preventable child and maternal deaths and ending extreme poverty. It is also in line with the goals articulated in the RBM Partnership's second generation global malaria action plan, *Action and Investment to defeat Malaria (AIM) 2016-2030: for a Malaria-Free World* and WHO's updated *Global Technical Strategy 2016-2030*. Under the PMI Strategy 2015-2020, the U.S. Government's goal is to work with PMI-supported countries and partners to further reduce malaria deaths and substantially decrease malaria morbidity, towards the long-term goal of elimination.

Mali was selected as a PMI focus country in FY 2007.

This FY 2016 Malaria Operational Plan presents a detailed implementation plan for Mali, based on the strategies of PMI and the National Malaria Control Program (NMCP). It was developed in consultation with the NMCP and with the participation of national and international partners involved in malaria prevention and control in the country. The activities that PMI is proposing to support fit in well with the National Malaria Control strategy and plan and build on investments made by PMI and other partners to improve and expand malaria-related services, including the Global Fund to Fight AIDS, Tuberculosis, and Malaria (Global Fund) malaria grants. This document briefly reviews the current status of malaria control policies and interventions in Mali, describes progress to date, identifies challenges and unmet needs to achieving the targets of the NMCP and PMI, and provides a description of activities that are planned with FY 2016 funding.

The proposed FY 2016 PMI budget for Mali is $25 million. PMI will support the following intervention areas with these funds:

Insecticide-treated nets (ITNs): The Malaria Strategic Plan promotes universal ITN coverage for all age groups (defined as one ITN for every two people). The MoH supports the provision of free ITNs distributed to target populations through two main delivery channels: mass distribution to households as part of universal coverage campaigns and routine distribution through antenatal care (ANC) and Expanded Program for Immunization clinics targeting pregnant women and infants. The NMCP has made significant progress recently toward achieving its initial goal of 80% use of ITNs among children under five and pregnant women. According to the recent 2012-2013 DHS conducted during the peak transmission season, 84% of households owned an ITN and 69% of children under five years of age and 73% of pregnant women slept under an ITN the previous night. Between 2014 and 2015, PMI supported mass distribution campaigns in the regions of Kayes and Koulikoro for their first rounds of the universal coverage campaign and the region of Sikasso for its second round to replace nets distributed in 2011. PMI also continued to support the routine distribution in collaboration with the Global Fund.

In FY 2016, PMI will procure 1.5 million nets that will be used for routine distribution to children and pregnant women in 2017. It is anticipated that the Global Fund will procure the needed nets for the mass campaigns to replace nets distributed in 2013 and 2014. PMI will continue to support BCC to maintain or increase the level of net use and educate people for care and repair.

Indoor residual spraying (IRS): PMI supports the NMCP's strategy to reduce malaria transmission through targeted IRS in select high-risk areas. Starting in 2008, PMI supported three IRS campaigns in the districts of Bla and Koulikoro, adding a third district (Baraoueli) in 2011. Support in 2014 included initial and refresher training of supervisors and spray operators as well as community health volunteers (*relais*); purchase of all commodities and personal protective equipment; and communication, supervision, monitoring, and environmental compliance activities. The 2014 IRS campaign covered approximately 229,000 houses, and protecting approximately 850,000 residents. With FY 2015 funding, PMI plans to reduce IRS to two districts given the added cost of moving to a new class of insecticide due to resistance. The district no longer covered by IRS will benefit from the full package of malaria control interventions, including seasonal malaria chemoprevention (SMC). With FY 2016 funds, PMI will continue to support IRS in two districts. In addition, PMI will also continue strengthening the MoH's capacity to plan and supervise IRS activities within the context of its integrated vector management strategy. Other support will go to entomological monitoring related to IRS, including insecticide monitoring, insecticide resistance testing, and overall implementation of the entomological monitoring plan.

Malaria in pregnancy (MIP): The 2012-2013 DHS showed an increase in the percentage of pregnant women who received the recommended two doses of sulfadoxine-pyrimethamine (SP) for intermittent preventive treatment for pregnant women (IPTp) at antenatal care visits during their pregnancy (from 4% in 2006 to 20% in 2012). Coverage of IPTp2 remains low despite high antenatal care attendance rates by pregnant women: 74% of pregnant women visit ANC at least once. With funds from FY 2012 and 2013, PMI procured 1.9 million SP treatments for IPTp. An MIP Working Group was established to revise the national guidelines to bring them in line with new WHO recommendations. Subsequently, 22 regional staff participated in a training of trainers to assist with the rollout of the new policy. Communications strategies on malaria in pregnancy have targeted religious leaders, traditional leaders, grandmothers, women in positions of authority, women of childbearing age, and men. With FY 2016 funding, PMI will procure 2 million SP treatments to help ensure that all pregnant women can receive at least three doses of IPTp administered as directly observed therapy. Through operational research programming, PMI will undertake a pilot of enhanced ANC and IPTp activities aimed at improving quality of ANC and increasing coverage of IPTp.

Case management: Poor geographic and economic access to care is a major challenge for malaria diagnosis and treatment in Mali. In 2010, due to advocacy efforts of PMI and other partners, the MoH adopted significant policy changes including a community case management policy and updated severe malaria treatment and pre-referral guidelines. As a result, routine health information systems data reports 90% of all suspected malaria cases were tested by microscopy or RDT in 2014, a significant improvement from 18% in 2010. PMI continued its support of the integrated community case management strategy in 2014 in five districts of Sikasso Region and expanded activities to four additional districts (two in Kayes Region and two in Segou Region). This support included training and deploying community health workers *(Agents de Santé Communautaire)*, procuring RDTs and ACTs for community-based diagnosis and treatment, and ensuring sufficient supplies of RDTs and ACTs for children under five years of age in health facilities. PMI has also procured drugs for the management of severe malaria as well as supported in-service training and supportive supervision of health workers and community health workers. In the 2013-2017 Malaria Strategic Plan, Mali introduced seasonal malaria chemoprevention (SMC) in selected districts targeting all children under five with four monthly rounds of a preventive treatment with SP and amodiaquine. In 2014, 21 of Mali's 64 districts were covered with SMC, including one in which PMI conducted an OR study to collect data on the feasibility and effectiveness of SMC under routine programmatic conditions. Due to a 3-year grant from UNITAID, SMC will be implemented in at least 42 districts during the 2015 and 2016 transmission seasons. Of the 42 districts, PMI will support the implementation in 10 districts in the focus regions of Kayes, Koulikoro, Sikasso, and Bamako.

With FY 2016 funding, PMI will continue to support and strengthen efforts to ensure prompt and effective case management of malaria at health facilities and support the scale-up of the integrated community case management policy nationwide. At the health facility level, PMI will concentrate on strengthening capacity in laboratory diagnostics (including quality assurance and quality control), and supply chain management. With the NMCP's scale up of SMC, PMI will support implementation of this new approach in 10 districts. PMI will procure 3 million RDTs and 850,000 million ACTs to contribute to filling gaps in annual malaria commodity needs for health facilities, integrated community case management, and SMC sites. PMI will strengthen quality assurance/quality control systems at national and district levels for accurate malaria diagnosis, and will support the NMCP to monitor and reinforce the correct use of ACTs at health facilities and in communities.

Health systems strengthening and capacity building: Since its first year, PMI has contributed substantially to building capacity of the NMCP and other Government of Mali entities. This support has allowed the government's partners to improve training, supervision, and quality assurance and quality control for diagnostics; to oversee implementation of BCC activities related to malaria; and to improve partner coordination. With the *coup* in 2012, PMI suspended direct funding for NMCP capacity-building efforts and focused on strengthening the health system at the community level. In 2013, the restrictions were lifted but direct funding to the NMCP is capped. With FY 2016 funding, PMI will support day-to-day operations through its implementing partners. These activities will include support for training, supervision, and infrastructure needed for optimal functioning. Collaboration will continue with other partners to support NMCP structure and staff, specifically to increase capacity at all levels for program management, including training, supervision, and facilitating forecasting and quantification for malaria commodities and training in logistic management information systems.

Behavior change communication (BCC): The NMCP developed a new BCC strategy for 2014-2018 with PMI support. The strategy describes BCC messages targeted to vulnerable groups including pregnant women and children under five as well as families and caretakers of children, community health workers, and *relais*. The national strategy supports multiple delivery channels for messages, including mass media and interpersonal communications. PMI supports harmonization of the national BCC strategy at all levels, ensuring consistency of messages and appropriate use of all communication channels. In FY 2015, the USAID/Mali Mission awarded a new BCC bilateral to work across all its health programs and PMI will channel its BCC work through that mechanism. Through this mechanism, PMI will support BCC activities at national and community levels to promote correct and consistent ITN use, especially among the most vulnerable groups. PMI will continue to support engagement and mobilization of pregnant women and the promotion of malaria in pregnancy and IPTp in the community through traditional leaders and midwives. PMI will support coordination and harmonization of work among implementing partners to ensure that effective BCC messages on prompt diagnosis and early case management of malaria are promoted and disseminated.

Monitoring and evaluation (M&E): The NMCP, with support from PMI and other partners, has developed a comprehensive national malaria monitoring and evaluation plan for 2013-2017, including capacity building, improvement of data collection, and provision of equipment to collect and analyze data. The quality of routine data collection, analysis and reporting through the health information system is variable and feedback is not delivered in a timely manner for program management.

With FY 2016 funds, PMI will expand its work to support the national health information system to strengthen the SLIS through training and supervision, with a focus on the community health center level (*Centres de Santé Communautaire*). Activities will broaden the reach of the system to new health districts and will expand the use of SMS technology to transfer data. Through training and supportive supervision, PMI will build capacity of local and regional health system staff to report and utilize surveillance data for epidemic detection and responding to epidemics in Mopti and the Northern Regions. PMI will support preliminary planning for the 2018 DHS to ensure that malaria indicators and interventions are incorporated into the survey.

Operational research (OR): Since 2008, OR has been conducted in Mali to answer specific questions regarding the implementation and effectiveness of critical malaria interventions. PMI has funded various studies such as: an evaluation of the expanded program on immunization to monitor bednet usage and treatment of childhood illnesses; the entomological impact of combining larviciding with IRS; and a cost analysis of removing user fees for children under five. With FY 2014 and FY 2015 funds, PMI supported two OR activities: (1) a study to evaluate the impact of ITNs treated with two insecticides to inform PMI about the potential ability of this new ITN variety to affect malaria transmission in areas with high pyrethroid resistance; and (2) an evaluation of the SMC intervention to determine its relative usefulness as part of the malaria control strategy in Mali. Using FY 2016 funding, PMI will evaluate the economics of health provider behavior as it relates to Mali's cost recovery system, in addition to evaluating an enhanced intervention package to improve uptake of IPTp.

II. STRATEGY

1. Introduction

When it was launched in 2005, the goal of PMI was to reduce malaria-related mortality by 50% across 15 high-burden countries in sub-Saharan Africa through a rapid scale-up of four proven and highly effective malaria prevention and treatment measures: insecticide-treated mosquito nets (ITNs); indoor residual spraying (IRS); accurate diagnosis and prompt treatment with artemisinin-based combination therapies (ACTs); and intermittent preventive treatment of pregnant women (IPTp). With the passage of the Tom Lantos and Henry J. Hyde Global Leadership against HIV/AIDS, Tuberculosis, and Malaria Act in 2008, PMI developed a U.S. Government Malaria Strategy for 2009–2014. This strategy included a long-term vision for malaria control in which sustained high coverage with malaria prevention and treatment interventions would progressively lead to malaria-free zones in Africa, with the ultimate goal of worldwide malaria eradication by 2040-2050. Consistent with this strategy and the increase in annual appropriations supporting PMI, four new sub-Saharan African countries and one regional program in the Greater Mekong Subregion of Southeast Asia were added in 2011. The contributions of PMI, together with those of other partners, have led to dramatic improvements in the coverage of malaria control interventions in PMI-supported countries, and all 15 original countries have documented substantial declines in all-cause mortality rates among children less than five years of age.

In 2015, PMI launched the next six-year strategy, setting forth a bold and ambitious goal and objectives. The PMI Strategy for 2015-2020 takes into account the progress over the past decade and the new challenges that have arisen. Malaria prevention and control remains a major U.S. foreign assistance objective and PMI's Strategy fully aligns with the U.S. Government's vision of ending preventable child and maternal deaths and ending extreme poverty. It is also in line with the goals articulated in the RBM Partnership's second generation global malaria action plan, *Action and Investment to defeat Malaria (AIM) 2016-2030: for a Malaria-Free World* and WHO's updated *Global Technical Strategy 2016-2030*. Under the PMI Strategy 2015-2020, the U.S. Government's goal is to work with PMI-supported countries and partners to further reduce malaria deaths and substantially decrease malaria morbidity, towards the long-term goal of elimination.

Mali was selected as a PMI focus country in FY 2007.

This FY 2016 Malaria Operational Plan presents a detailed implementation plan for Mali, based on the strategies of PMI and the National Malaria Control Program (NMCP) strategy. It was developed in consultation with the NMCP and with the participation of national and international partners involved in malaria prevention and control in the country. The activities that PMI is proposing to support fit in well with the National Malaria Control strategy and plan and build on investments made by PMI and other partners to improve and expand malaria-related services, including the Global Fund to Fight AIDS, Tuberculosis, and Malaria (Global Fund) malaria grants. This document briefly reviews the current status of malaria control policies and interventions in Mali, describes progress to date, identifies challenges and unmet needs to achieving the targets of the NMCP and PMI, and provides a description of activities that are planned with FY 2016 funding.

2. Malaria situation in Mali

Malaria is the primary cause of morbidity and mortality in Mali, particularly for children less than five years old. In 2014, the national health information system (*Système Local d'Information Sanitaire* or [SLIS]) reported 2.5 million clinical cases of malaria in health facilities, accounting for 40% of all outpatient visits for all age groups. A total of 2,280 fatal malaria cases were reported. However, SLIS data should be viewed with caution due to its variable quality. According to the 2012 Demographic and Health Survey (DHS), the prevalence of malaria among children under five years of age was 52% based on microscopy and 47% based on rapid diagnostic tests (RDTs).

Plasmodium falciparum accounts for 85-90% of malaria infections, while *P. malariae* (10-14%) and *P. ovale* (1%) make up the remainder. A 2004 study conducted by the Malaria Research and Training Center (MRTC) in Menaka, an epidemic-prone region in the north, indicated a prevalence of *P. vivax* of 8%, which was confirmed by polymerase chain reaction.

Malaria is endemic to the central and southern regions, where about 90% of Mali's population lives, and it is epidemic in the north due to the limited viability of *Anopheles* species in the desert climate. Malaria transmission varies in Mali's five geoclimatic zones. It occurs year-round in the Sudano-Guinean zone in the south, with a seasonal peak between June and November. The transmission season is shorter in the northern Sahelian zone, lasting approximately three to four months (July/August to October). Malaria transmission is endemic in the Niger River Delta and areas around dams with rice cultivation, and is endemic with low transmission in urban areas including Bamako and Mopti. Epidemics occur in the north (Tombouctou, Gao, and Kidal Regions) and in the northern districts of Kayes, Koulikoro, Segou, and Mopti regions; the last epidemic was identified by the MoH and WHO in November 2012 in Tombouctou.

Figure 1. Average rainfall density in millimeters, Mali, 2007 to 2013

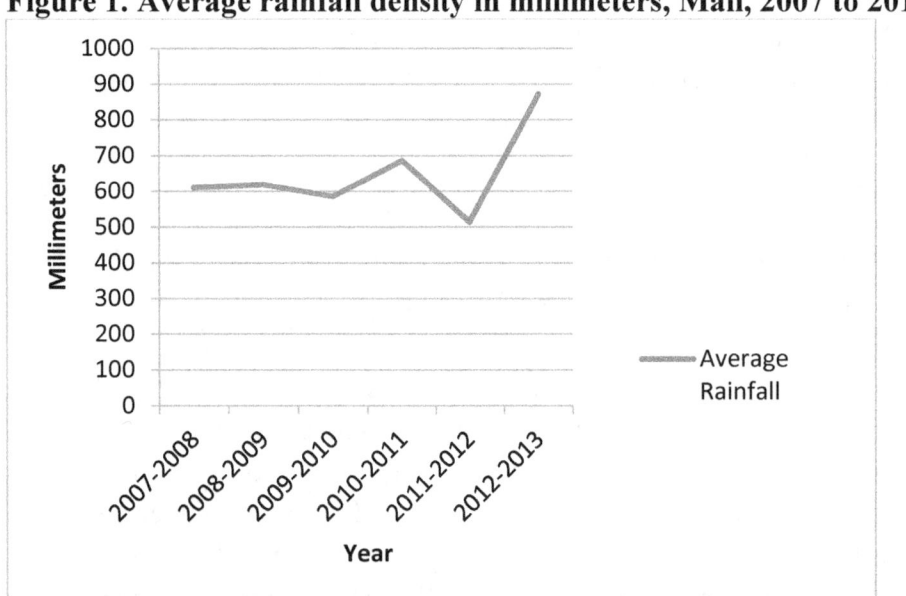

Source: Agence Nationale de la Météorologie – Mali-Météo
Note: Rainfall ranges from 62mm in Aguelhoc in 2011 (Kidal Region) to 1,377mm in Kolondieba (Sikasso Region) in 2012. In 2012, the country registered record-setting rainfall; this may partially explain the high prevalence of parasitemia observed during the 2012 DHS.

Figure 2. Under-five malaria prevalence with microscopy (DHS 2012-2013)

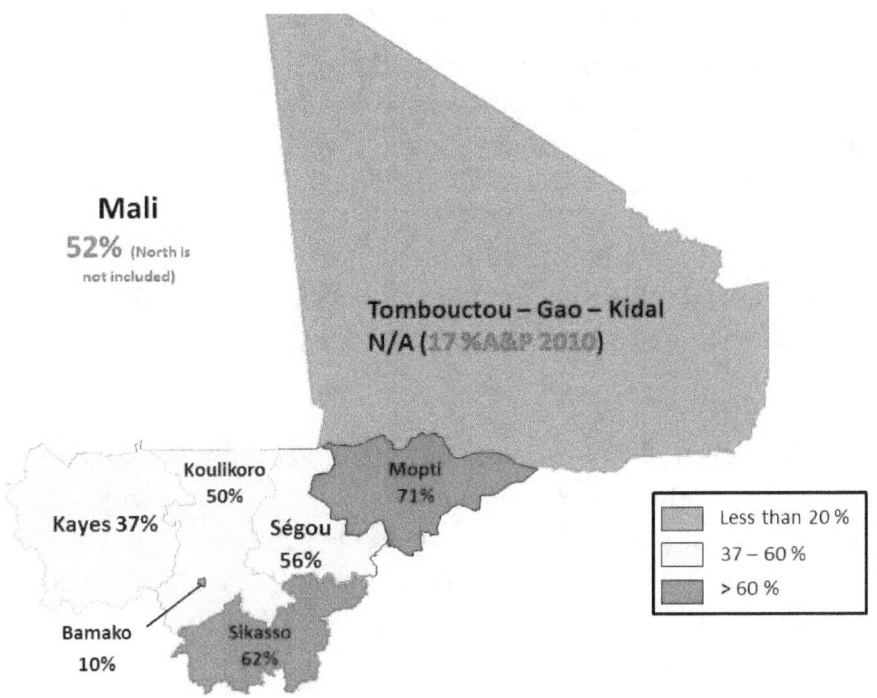

3. Country health system delivery structure and Ministry of Health (MoH) organization

At the national level, Mali's MoH is composed of the cabinet of the Minister of Health and National Directorates reporting directly to the Secretary General of the MoH. The NMCP was established in 1993 under the oversight of the Disease Control Division of the National Health Directorate. In July 2007, the Government of Mali (GoM) elevated the NMCP to a directorate level in the MoH organizational structure. The NMCP is composed of four technical divisions and one administrative and finance division, and the director reports directly to the secretary general of the MoH. Due to its higher profile in the MoH, the NMCP can participate in and influence decision-making about malaria control more effectively, including development of MoH work plans and budgets.

Mali is divided into eight administrative regions (Kayes, Koulikoro, Sikasso, Ségou, Mopti, Gao, Tombouctou, and Kidal) plus the capital, Bamako. Each represents a regional health directorate. The regions are subdivided into 49 administrative "*cercles*" (or communes) comprised of 58 health districts, and Bamako is divided into six administrative communes that correspond to six health districts; thus the country has a total of 64 health districts. Governance is decentralized into 703 communes (19 rural and 684 urban), each one administered by an elected local council headed by a mayor. The organization of the health system is based upon the principles of decentralization of health services and community participation to extend health service coverage and to ensure access to essential and effective medicines.

The health delivery system is composed of three levels:

- The <u>central level</u> with five national reference hospitals
- The <u>intermediate level</u> with eight regional hospitals (Kayes, Kati, Sikasso, Ségou, Mopti, Tombouctou, Gao, and the maternal and child hospital of Bamako)
- The <u>local level</u> with 64 referral health centers (*Centres de Santé de Référence* [CSREF]) constituting the district reference level

As of December 2014, a total of 1,206 functional community health centers (*Centres de Santé Communautaire* [CSCOM]) as well as parastatal, faith-based, military, and other private health centers, make up the community health services level. The CSCOMs are established and managed by community health associations.

The MoH has a critical staff shortage at all levels of the public health system, especially for service provision below the national level. In addition, health workers are not distributed proportionally to population throughout the country. In 2014, the national ratio of doctors to the population was 1/8,528, (WHO recommends 1/10,000) but rural regions have less than one doctor for every 24,000 inhabitants. Regional directors oversee health teams that implement integrated health interventions; currently all regional teams have malaria focal persons. The CSREF (at the district level) is the first referral structure for CSCOMs; the district health team is headed by a medical chief responsible for technical supervision of CSCOMs and has a malaria focal person as well. The community health associations manage CSCOM staff and operations; collect proceeds from drug sales, consultations, and user fees; and pay salaries and other expenses. As is the case at the central level, distribution of staff is uneven. In 2009, the percentage of CSCOMs headed by a certified head nurse was close to the World Health Organization (WHO) norms and ranged from 100% in five regions to 95% in Kayes. According to the strategic plan for health and social development (2014-2023), in 2011, 30% of CSCOMs were headed by a medical doctor. The number of staff employed depends on the level of community resources to pay them. In 2011, the MoH started the "medicalization" of CSCOMs, meaning the appointment of qualified medical doctors in CSCOMs.

In 2010, Mali approved an integrated community case management (iCCM) package offered by community health workers (*Agents de Santé Communautaires* [ASCs]) to provide health services at the village and household levels. The ASCs, who receive a financial incentive or salaries from the local government and different partners for their services, provide free treatment for uncomplicated malaria and malnutrition, with payment for treatment of acute respiratory infections, and diarrhea. The ASCs also provide primary care to newborns and family planning for eligible families. Based on national iCCM directives, the iCCM package and ASC model has been introduced in villages located 5 km or more from a health facility and covers 2-3 villages in a radius of 3 km with a catchment area of approximately 1,500 people. This iCCM approach and ASC efforts are supported by an additional cadre of community health volunteers, the *relais*, whose role is to carry out behavior change communication activities (BCC) and health education to promote key health messages to complement iCCM activities. Support for the GoM scale-up plan for nationwide implementation of the iCCM package including supervision, commodity management, RDT confirmation, and quality assurance/quality control (QA/QC) were incorporated into the Global Fund to Fight AIDS, Tuberculosis, and Malaria (Global Fund) consolidated grant. As of June 2014, a total of 2,317 ASCs had been trained and are fully functional; an estimated 4,876 ASCs are needed to achieve full coverage of iCCM activities. The iCCM *ad hoc* group is developing a plan where each donor partner will indicate the number of ASCs to be supported by the partner and in which geographic area.

Mali has a strong cost recovery system that is based on the Bamako Initiative. At the district level, communities can establish CSCOMs based on the following criteria: the establishment of a community health association; raising a minimum of 10% of the cost of construction or renovation of the health facility; and the hiring and support of health personnel. All CSCOMs are required to deliver the national minimum package of services comprising curative, preventive, and promotional health activities. Once authorized by the district medical officer, the MoH provides an initial stock of medicines, consumables, and equipment. In principle, communes are expected to allocate 15% of their budget for social services including water, education, and health.

CSCOMs have three forms of revenue generation that are managed by the community health association: membership fees, sales of essential drugs, and fees for services. Service fees vary by health area and are set by the community health association after consultation with the population. Membership fees allow for reduced service charges at some CSCOMs. Funds derived from the sale of medications are kept in a separate account to prevent providers from overprescribing to generate revenue and to prevent decapitalization of pharmacy stock. The community health association management committee purchases replacement drugs for the CSCOM through the national pharmacy system or from approved private sector companies based on availability. Selected drugs (e.g., antimalarials for children under five and pregnant women, vitamin A, and immunization services) are provided free by the government or donors. The CSCOMs must finance the transportation of their drugs from CSREFs. However, due to small profit margins and the loss of or use of revenues for non-pharmaceutical purposes, CSCOM drug stores often lack available funds to cover these costs.

National financial planning for malaria and health/social development

The NMCP receives annual budget support from the National Health and Social Development Program. Its Evaluation Committee manages and approves the annual operating budget plan. Several partners (including the governments of the Netherlands, Sweden, and Canada) provide direct budget support on an annual basis. Other donors, including the USG, target their funding to sub-sectors and specific programs. The GoM contributes mostly to salaries, office space, and other operating costs in the program's annual budget, but also procures malaria commodities such as artemisinin-based combination therapy (ACTs), rapid diagnostic tests (RDTs), severe malaria drugs, seasonal malaria chemoprevention (SMC) drugs, and insecticide-treated mosquito nets (ITNs). The GoM, local governments, community health associations and other donor partners, such as the Global Alliance for Vaccines and Immunizations (GAVI) are supporting the salaries of CSCOM staff, including qualified medical doctors. While the GoM increased its annual investment in malaria control from about $1 million in FY 2007 to $6.7 million in FY 2008 and $9 million in FY 2009, this support decreased to approximately $4 million in FY 2010 and $3 million in FY 2011. The GoM budget for malaria remained $2.5 million per year from 2012 to 2015.

4. National malaria control strategy

The NMCP establishes strategies for all malaria interventions; coordinates research; proposes policies, norms, and guidelines; and coordinates partner work plans. The NMCP also supports decentralized regional and district health teams through training and supervision. In 2013, a five-year strategic plan (2013–2017) was developed and published by the NMCP and partners. Its goal is to "reduce the burden of malaria to a level that will not constitute a major cause of morbidity and mortality nor a barrier to economic and social development."

The new NMCP Strategic Plan aims to achieve the following targets by 2017:

- Reduce malaria mortality to near zero
- Reduce malaria morbidity by at least 75% as compared to 2000 levels
- Reinforce/strengthen the NMCP coordination and management capacity

Expected results to be achieved by the 2013-2017 strategic plan are as follows:

- At least 80% of the population at risk of malaria is using ITNs, including pregnant women and children under five years old;
- At least 80% of pregnant women have received three sulfadoxine-pyrimethamine (SP) doses as intermittent preventive treatment for pregnant women (IPTp) during their pregnancy;
- At least 80% of children under five received the four full courses of seasonal malaria chemoprevention (SMC) in selected zones;
- At least 90% of suspected malaria cases are confirmed using microscopy or RDTs before treatment, at all levels of the health system including the ASC level;
- At least 90% of confirmed malaria cases receive appropriate malaria treatment both for severe and uncomplicated cases as indicated in the national guidelines;
- At least 80% of the population is protected by indoor residual spraying (IRS) in IRS target zones;
- At least 80% of the general population knows what interventions are recommended to prevent malaria;
- At least 90% of emergency cases and malaria epidemics are detected within two weeks and receive an appropriate response.

Due to the diversity of malaria transmission in Mali (largely endemic in the south and epidemic-prone in the north), the strategic plan emphasizes nationwide universal coverage of key malaria interventions for prevention and control of malaria, as well as specific interventions such as epidemic and entomological surveillance and targeted operational research in areas with unstable malaria transmission. Below are the main intervention areas with their strategic approach:

- Access to and use of ITNs through 1) routine distribution to pregnant women at their first antenatal care (ANC) visit and to children under one year of age at their measles vaccination visit through the expanded programme on immunization (EPI), and 2) through phased mass distribution campaigns (region-by-region) defined as one net for every two persons;

- IPTp for pregnant women with sulfadoxine pyrimethamine (SP) given as direct observed treatment (DOT) monthly following the first trimester to achieve three doses or more of SP during pregnancy;
- SMC using sulfadoxine-pyrethamine/amodiaquine (SP/AQ) in children aged 3-59 months during the peak transmission period (August – November);
- Indoor residual spraying in targeted, high burden areas using organophosphates insecticides during the raining season;
- Case management by diagnosing suspect malaria cases through microscopy or RDT, and treatment of confirmed positive cases using artemisinin-based combination therapy (ACT). The first-line treatment for uncomplicated malaria is artemether-lumefantrine (AL) and artesunate-amodiaquine (AS/AQ) as second-line. Injectable artesunate is used for severe malaria cases. To ensure correct case management, the GoM decided that RDTs should be free for everybody and treatment with ACTs is free for pregnant women and children under five years old at all levels of the health pyramid including the community level;
- Strengthen the sentinel surveillance systems (epidemiological and entomological) in areas with unstable malaria transmission;
- Strengthen the integrated disease surveillance system in all districts and hospitals to collect weekly malaria data for prompt decision making;
- Strengthen behavior change communication (BCC) in order to increase the appropriate use of ITNs and promote early care seeking for patients with fever and encourage early ANC attendance by pregnant women;
- Revitalize monitoring and evaluation (M&E) and surveillance interventions by strengthening the routine surveillance system at all levels of the health system;
- Strengthen operational research through studies and surveys on malaria;
- Revitalize and strengthen the national Roll Back Malaria (RBM) partnership to leverage sustainable funds for malaria activities;
- Reinforce regional malaria coordination and collaboration; and
- Reinforce managerial capacity of the NMCP and coordination mechanisms at all levels of the health pyramid.

5. Updates in the strategy section

The following are updates to the strategy section of this document for FY 2016.

- A Global Fund Concept Note was submitted in April 2015 which would provide approximately 48 million Euros for essential malaria commodities and services.
- The SMC program will expand beyond its pilot phase in 2015 to cover 41 districts out of 64 in the country.
- Mali was affected by the 2014 Ebola outbreak which slowed progress on a number of malaria activities as resources were reassigned to combatting Ebola.

- Subsequent to the Ebola epidemic, Mali has been identified as one of 30 countries to benefit from the Global Health Security Agenda (GHSA) funding. These funds will be used to target many areas of mutual concern with malaria programming, such as surveillance, laboratory, and outbreak response capacity, and health systems strengthening.
- USAID/Mali has identified four regions (Koulikoro, Sikasso, Kayes, and Bamako) as priority regions for its bilateral interventions. PMI activities run through bilateral projects will focus on those four regions. However, the PMI program provides national support to the NMCP and will also provide commodities and do limited implementation of activities nationwide.

6. Integration, collaboration, and coordination

Communications among malaria control partners in Mali are coordinated through the NMCP monthly partners' meetings. Malaria control is part of the national sector-wide approach, based on a strategic Ten-Year Plan for Social and Health Development and operationalized through the five-year National Health and Social Development Program. The plan is supported by the Financial and Technical Partners' Forum, which meets monthly to share information on ongoing programs, new initiatives, strategies, and policies; to coordinate interventions; and to help leverage resources. The NMCP is responsible for overseeing all malaria control activities conducted in Mali, but donor coordination needs to be strengthened.

Funding

Key funding and technical partners to the NCMP include the Global Fund, WHO, UNICEF, the World Bank, and the USG. The U.S. National Institutes of Health also supports the MRTC within the Faculty of Medicine at the University of Bamako. At the implementation level, partners include numerous nongovernmental and private voluntary organizations including *Groupe Pivot Santé*, the National Federation of Community Health Associations (*Fédération Nationale des Associations de Santé Communautaire)*, Doctors without Borders (*Médecins Sans Frontières)*, World Vision, and Plan International. Partner funding activities include the following:

- UNICEF implements iCCM in 30 health districts
- The Muskoka Initiative, funded by the Canadian International Development Agency (CIDA), is implementing iCCM in four districts in the Sikasso Region that are not already covered by PMI
- WHO provides technical assistance in malaria with the development of Global Fund proposals and the development of new NMCP and MoH policy and strategy documents
- Catholic Relief Services (CRS) will be expanding SMC in Mali with UNITAID funds. An average of more than 866,000 children under five of age will be covered with SMC in 2015.

The approved Global Fund Round 10 malaria grant and the Round 6 Phase 2 grant have been consolidated into one malaria grant, which was signed in May 2013. The consolidated malaria grant supports scaling up iCCM implementation, procurement of ACTs and RDTs, and support for a universal ITN coverage campaign in 2015 in Bamako. The total budget amount under this grant is approximately $60 million for the first three years.

In April 2015, Mali submitted a malaria concept note to the Global Fund. If approved, this grant of approximately 48 million Euros will cover malaria prevention interventions from January 2016 to December 2018. Activities outlined in this grant will continue the scale-up of SMC, iCCM, procurement of ACTs and RDTs, and support for a universal ITN coverage campaign.

Other USG programs

Malaria prevention and control is a major foreign assistance objective of the USG. The U.S. Agency for International Development (USAID)/Mali supports a number of programs of the MoH including family planning, maternal and child health, nutrition, and water/sanitation programs. Through this diverse array of programs, USAID has contributed considerably to the strengthening of the Malian health system.

As a USG Feed the Future country (2011–2016), Mali is implementing a coordinated government strategy to address food security and nutrition issues. Anemia, due to iron deficiency, malaria, and helminth infections, affects over 80% of children under five nationwide and exceeds 90% in some regions (e.g., Sikasso). The GoM is committed to developing multi-sectorial programs that address access to health care to improve overall dietary intake and disease status of Malians. PMI is working in collaboration with Feed the Future and GHI to improve maternal and child health services and coordinate on relevant malaria and nutrition BCC messages.

The Ebola epidemic in West Africa highlights the urgency for immediate action to establish global capacity to prevent, detect, and rapidly respond to biological threats like Ebola. The Global Health Security Agenda was launched in February 2014 to advance a world safe and secure from infectious disease threats and to bring together nations from all over the world to make new, concrete commitments, and to elevate global health security as a national leaders-level priority. The USG committed to assist at least 30 countries, including Mali, over five years to strengthen the health system to prevent outbreaks, detect threats in real time and rapidly respond to infectious diseases.

PMI and GHSA remain in constant contact in coordinating efforts towards health system strengthening. PMI/Mali has been involved in participating in the GHSA scoping visits to ensure complementary activities, and to share PMI practices, lessons learned, and strengths in prevention, detection, and response efforts. Specifically, there are currently three priority areas that PMI has been involved in with regards to Mali's 18-month operational plan. Priority 1 includes developing a plan to incrementally strengthen capacity from national to regional to district levels on policies and strategies related to HMIS, rapid response, surveillance, and laboratory systems. Priority 2 encourages strengthening workforce development through training cohorts of health district staff in basic and intermediate epidemiology short courses through the Field Epidemiology and Laboratory Training Program (FELTP). Priority 3 will use the Hajj pilgrimage infrastructure, and expand the Ebola incident management system to implement and evaluate surveillance and laboratory capacity, and data management systems to address GHS activities related to the three selected syndromes (AHF, SARS, watery diarrhea and dehydration). PMI is investing in HMIS and surveillance, and will continue to leverage GHSA for additional funding. PMI will also benefit from a well trained workforce such as FELTP staff to conduct some malaria surveillance activities.

Private sector partnerships

The NMCP and PMI maintain working relationships with several members of the private sector, including the recent partnership with the Association of Employers and Business Owners (*Patronnat du Mali*) and the bank sector. With the country's well-established net culture, mosquito net vendors in Mali enjoy a large market in both urban and rural areas. The NMCP has a long-established collaboration with mosquito net vendors in Mali. Private clinics, pharmacies, and laboratories are becoming more prevalent with a larger presence in urban areas. The NMCP, with support from PMI, conducted an assessment of the private pharmacies' performance in malaria treatment and the NMCP is developing an action plan to improve case management at this level including the testing of suspected cases before prescribing an ACT. To date, the NMCP has provided them with malaria case management information based on country guidelines. The NMCP plans to train and supervise private sector personnel to ensure the national directives related to malaria diagnostics and treatment are understood and applied. PMI and the USAID/Mali Mission will support efforts to strengthen medical practices within private pharmacies, including testing and treating for malaria.

The mining industry is growing in Mali. Currently, at least five mining companies are supporting IRS activities in their employees' residence sites and neighboring villages. PMI will continue to facilitate a dialogue between the NMCP and the mining companies to ensure that they adhere to national and international IRS standards and to promote best practices, such as entomological surveillance.

7. PMI goal, objectives, strategic areas, and key indicators

Under the PMI Strategy for 2015-2020, the U.S. Government's goal is to work with PMI-supported countries and partners to further reduce malaria deaths and substantially decrease malaria morbidity, towards the long-term goal of elimination. Building upon the progress to date in PMI-supported countries, PMI will work with NMCPs and partners to accomplish the following objectives by 2020:

1. Reduce malaria mortality by one-third from 2015 levels in PMI-supported countries, achieving a greater than 80% reduction from PMI's original 2000 baseline levels.

2. Reduce malaria morbidity in PMI-supported countries by 40% from 2015 levels.

3. Assist at least five PMI-supported countries to meet the World Health Organization's (WHO) criteria for national or sub-national pre-elimination.[1]

These objectives will be accomplished by emphasizing five core areas of strategic focus:

1. Achieving and sustaining scale of proven interventions

---

[1] http://whqlibdoc.who.int/publications/2007/9789241596084_eng.pdf

2. Adapting to changing epidemiology and incorporating new tools
3. Improving countries' capacity to collect and use information
4. Mitigating risk against the current malaria control gains
5. Building capacity and health systems towards full country ownership

To track progress toward achieving and sustaining scale of proven interventions (area of strategic focus #1), PMI will continue to track the key indicators recommended by the Roll Back Malaria Monitoring and Evaluation Reference Group (RBM MERG) as listed below:

- Proportion of households with at least one ITN
- Proportion of households with at least one ITN for every two people
- Proportion of children under five years old who slept under an ITN the previous night
- Proportion of pregnant women who slept under an ITN the previous night
- Proportion of households in targeted districts protected by IRS
- Proportion of children under five years old with fever in the last two weeks for whom advice or treatment was sought
- Proportion of children under five with fever in the last two weeks who had a finger or heel stick
- Proportion receiving an ACT among children under five years old with fever in the last two weeks who received any antimalarial drugs
- Proportion of women who received two or more doses of IPTp for malaria during ANC visits during their last pregnancy

8. Progress on coverage/impact indicators to date

Since PMI's launch in 2007 in Mali, impressive gains in child survival have been noticed; all-cause under-five-mortality fell from 191 deaths per 1,000 live births in 2006 DHS to 95 deaths per 1,000 live births in the 2012-2013 DHS. This represents a reduction of under-five deaths by 50%. Since malaria is the number one cause of mortality among children under five, these results are likely due to the success of malaria control efforts. The results from the 2012-2013 DHS show mixed evidence of progress for the malaria control program. Coverage of key interventions has remained steady since 2010 and, in some cases, increased despite the political turmoil of 2012/2013. Household ownership of ITNs remained constant at 84%, one of the highest coverage levels among PMI focus countries and a major achievement given the instability in the country. ITN use among children under five also remained steady at 69%, while use among pregnant women increased from 55% in 2010 to 73% in 2012. There was likewise an increase in the percentage of women receiving two doses of IPTp from 4% in 2006 to 20% in 2012. In terms of impact, the percentage of children with severe anemia (<8g/dl) fell from 26% in 2010 to 20.6% in 2012.

However, the same survey's preliminary figures on parasitemia indicate an increase in prevalence from 38% in 2010 to 52% in 2012. There are many hypotheses as to why the high levels of coverage have not translated to reductions in parasitemia in this age group. Mali experienced record-setting rainfall in 2012 just prior to the field work for the survey which may have acted as a catalyst to transmission. In addition, the sampling frame for the anemia and parasitemia survey included the low-transmission regions of the North in the denominator, whereas the DHS 2012-2013 excluded the North because of the instability. Thus, the higher level of parasitemia in 2012 might be partially derived from a difference in sampling frames between the two surveys. Finally, the high transmission zones of southern Mali have seen an influx of internally displaced persons (IDPs) from the low malaria burden areas of the North. These IDPs do not have acquired immunity to malaria and may exhibit higher parasite prevalence.

Table 1: Evolution of Key Malaria Indicators in Mali from 2006 to 2015

Indicator	2006 DHS	2010 AP Survey[*]	2012-2013 DHS**	Other data sources
% Households with at least one ITN	50%	85%	84%	NA
% Households with at least one ITN for every two people	NA	NA	NA	NA
% Children under five who slept under an ITN the previous night	27%	70%	69%	NA
% Pregnant women who slept under an ITN the previous night	29%	NA	73%	55% (MICS 2010)
% Households in targeted districts protected by IRS	NA	NA	NA	98% (2013 Abt EOSR)
% Children under five years old with fever in the last two weeks for whom advice or treatment was sought	NA	8%	32%	NA
% Children under five with fever in the last two weeks who had a finger or heel stick	NA	NA	12%	NA
% Children receiving an ACT among children under five years old with fever in the last two weeks who received any antimalarial drugs	NA	8%	19%	NA
% Women who received two or more doses of IPTp during their last pregnancy in the last two years	4%	NA	20%	32% (HMIS 2012)
Any anemia (<11g/dL)	81%	85%	82%	NA
Severe anemia (<8g/dL)	10%	26%	20%	NA
Parasite prevalence (microscopy/RDT)	NA	38%/43%	52%/47%	NA

[*]AP: Anemia and Parasitemia
**National estimate that excludes the lower-prevalence northern region.

9. Other relevant evidence on progress

In 2014, PMI funded an OR study to evaluate the effectiveness of delivering SMC as compared to standard malaria case management through existing community health workers. A non-randomized pre-post design was used, where the intervention district (Kita) received four rounds of SMC with SP+AQ, while the comparison district (Bafoulabé) received standard care. Children aged 3-59 months were included in the study. In addition to a pre-post survey, blood smears were collected to measure parasitemia and hemoglobin. Difference-in-differences regression models were used to assess and compare changes in malaria and anemia in the intervention and comparison districts.

During round one, 84% of targeted children received at least the first SMC dose, but coverage declined to 67% by round four. Across the four treatment rounds, 54% of children received four complete SMC courses. Prevalence of parasitemia and malaria disease (fever + parasitemia) was similar in intervention (23.4%) and control (29.5%) districts prior to SMC (p=0.34). After SMC, parasitemia prevalence fell to 18% in the intervention district and increased to 46% in the control district (Difference-in-differences (DD) OR=0.35; 95% CI: 0.20-0.60). SMC also significantly reduced the odds of malaria disease (DD OR=0.20; 95% CI: 0.04-0.94) and moderate anemia (Hb<8 g/dL) (DD OR=0.26, 95% CI: 0.11-0.65).

Routine implementation of SMC in Mali substantially reduced malaria and anemia, with reductions of similar magnitude to those seen in in clinical pilots of the intervention. Improving coverage could further strengthen SMC impact.

10. Challenges and opportunities

Challenges

Recent political and security instability, NMCP capacity, and challenges in coordinating donor funding, threaten Malians' access to malaria prevention and treatment interventions. The situation in Mali is dynamic, however, and with a thorough understanding of these challenges, PMI can leverage resources, both technical and financial, to address these threats.

Security in the northern regions of Gao, Tomboutou, and Kidal is the primary challenge to implementing malaria control and prevention activities to a population with low immunity and limited access to health care. Due to the instability in the north, data to monitor malaria indicators were not collected during the 2012 – 2013 DHS, routine HMIS was discontinued during the period of occupation by rebel groups, and the 2015 MIS will not be conducted in the north. Although the situation has improved considerably after the rebels were driven out by international forces and with the progressive installation of Malian authorities in the northern regions, residual resurrections of rebel activities are spreading to the central regions of Mopti and Segou and continue to be a challenge for the full implementation of some basic services. The country anticipates that as the region stabilizes, proposed activities, such as epidemic surveillance and response (ESR), can be resumed.

Another challenge is the Ebola situation in the West African Region which affected Mali in 2014. The country registered eight Ebola cases including six fatal cases. Ministry of Health staff and frontline health workers in affected regions, including community health workers were fully engaged in the Ebola response. Consequently, many other health activities received very limited attention during this critical time.

Mali has long had exceptional laboratory capacity thanks to a long (20+ years) affiliation with NIH as a Center of Excellence. When Ebola started in Guinea, Mali was able to update this laboratory so that Ebola testing could be done in Mali. This was one of the keys to the successful containment of Ebola Virus Disease (EVD). Whereas other countries waited for days to have results from external laboratories, Mali was able to perform Ebola tests in-country and get a result in few hours.

- When EVD first occurred in neighboring countries, Mali developed a contingency plan which had two components: one plan without EVD and another one in case of EVD. Mali had the benefit of a time lag from the first notifications in Guinea and later Senegal, before cases were actually detected in Mali.
- CDC and USAID provided critical technical assistance from Atlanta and Washington. This technical assistance made a difference.
- The CDC Director called the Malian President to provide advice and told him to set up an emergency operations center and appoint an Ebola focal point.
- When the first case of Ebola started in Mali, members of the High-risk Countries Team, who were already in-country participating in a WHO EVD Preparedness mission, assisted Mali MoH staff with the response by drafting standard operating procedures and contact tracing and BCC guidelines, and helping to institute an incident command structure.
- UNICEF, WHO, MINISMA, local and international NGOs used qualified staff who worked in Guinea, Liberia, and Sierra Leone and came up with lessons learned from those highly affected countries to finalized Mali Ebola response strategy.
- Mali has good coordination mechanisms which contributed to making a difference.

The Government of Mali (GoM) and its partners successfully contained the Ebola epidemic and on January 18, 2014 the country was declared Ebola free.

The NMCP has several administrative and managerial issues to resolve, including:

- Inadequate office space and unreliable electricity supply and internet connectivity;
- Inefficient supply chain management systems where malaria drugs are often available at national and regional levels but not at the health facilities and community levels;
- Difficulty coordinating multiple donor partners with different agendas;
- Despite some progress in routine system strengthening, the quality and use of HMIS data still has major issues including timeliness, completeness, and accuracy, and data are not routinely used to inform decision-making.

The Mali team has taken these challenges into consideration during the FY 2016 MOP planning process. Proposed activities seek to address these issues, including continued M&E support for routine system strengthening, supply chain management, and continued implementation of iCCM to increase community access to health care. PMI has also reprogrammed some FY 2014 funds to further support the NMCP to support the monitoring of malaria activities in the field and allow continued electricity supply.

Opportunities

New opportunities have also been identified to contribute to significantly improve the malaria situation in Mali:

- A Concept Note for the Global Fund New Funding Model has been developed in the amount of 48 million Euros for three years. In addition to the procurement of common malaria commodities, this grant includes an important health systems strengthening component including monitoring and evaluation, with support to the HMIS and logistics management information systems, community health systems, and capacity building.
- Mali is the recipient of the UNITAID-funded ACCESS-SMC initiative to implement seasonal malaria chemoprevention in 24 districts including procurement of SMC drugs and support for operational costs. This will allow expansion of the SMC program to 42 districts covering approximately 2.7 million children.
- With the USG's commitment through the Global Health Security Agenda, Mali will have the opportunity over the next five years (2015-2020) to strengthen its health system, and be better prepared for immediate infectious disease threats.

III. OPERATIONAL PLAN

PMI will support the NMCP and its key objective of reducing the burden of malaria by filling commodity gaps and ensuring the availability of ITNs, RDTs, ACTs, and SP at the local level and bolstering the supply chain system to avoid future stockouts. PMI will continue to support the implementation of IRS in two districts and iCCM, and SMC in USAID/Mali's four intervention regions (Kayes, Koulikoro, Sikasso, and the district of Bamako). PMI funds will be used to update and develop skills in diagnostics and case management among providers, principally at the community levels, but also throughout the health system. The overall health system will be strengthened through improved approaches to monitoring and evaluation, including enhancements to the routine HMIS and training of health care providers and managers on use of data for decision-making. Operational research activities will be undertaken to fine tune program implementation for the Malian context. Finally, all the service provision improvements will be supported through a strong BCC program to improve knowledge about malaria control in the communities.

1. Insecticide-treated nets

NMCP/PMI objectives

The MoH supports the provision of free ITNs distributed to target populations through two main delivery channels: mass distribution to households as part of universal coverage campaigns and routine distribution through antenatal care (ANC) and child immunization clinics. Mali defines achievement of universal coverage as one ITN for every two persons. Since 2007, the MoH provided free ITNs to children under five years of age in an integrated campaign and through a phased national universal coverage campaign for all susceptible populations. To sustain coverage, the MoH provides free nets to pregnant women at their first ANC visit and to infants when they complete their national immunization series.

Progress since PMI was launched

Traditionally Mali has had a strong culture of net ownership and use as shown by the "Culture of Net Use Survey" conducted in 2013; ownership of at least one net per household is high and the use of nets in the vulnerable population is even higher. According to the 2012/2013 DHS survey conducted during the peak transmission season, 84% of households owned at least one ITN and 69% of children under five and 73% of pregnant women slept under a ITN the previous night. These findings suggest that Mali has not only maintained high net ownership since December 2007, but has increased coverage. Following its adoption of universal coverage, Mali launched a rolling, phased campaign in April 2011 to achieve 100% ownership and 80% use of ITNs in the general population. The NMCP and partners opted for a phased approach to the campaign, starting with the region of Sikasso in 2011, and then covering the regions of Segou, Mopti, Kayes, and Koulikoro from 2012 to 2014. The District of Bamako will receive nets during the June 2015 campaign. The mass distribution campaign in the three regions of the north (Gao, Tombouctou, and Kidal) initially planned for 2015 was postponed for security reasons and is now anticipated for 2016 as security permits. An estimated 8.67 million nets were originally needed based on a population of 15.6 million for one round. As of April 2015, more than 7,464,116 ITNs were distributed in 5 of 9 regions, of which PMI provided more than 6 million ITNs.

Progress during the last 12-18 months

During the last 12 to 18 months, PMI distributed 2,852,200 nets as part of the rolling campaign in the regions of Kayes, Koulikoro, and the remaining two districts in the Mopti Region that were not covered initially because of insecurity during the rebellion crisis. Additionally, PMI procured and distributed 2,089,789 nets for ANC and EPI routine distribution.

On May 30, 2015, PMI and the Global Fund launched the second round of a mass campaign in the region of Sikasso to replace nets distributed in 2011 – around 1.7 million nets were procured of which PMI contributed 900,000 and Global Fund 800,000 nets. PMI is supporting the distribution costs for the entire 1.7 million nets. In June 2015, the Global Fund will distribute 1.7 million nets to achieve universal coverage in the six communes of Bamako the capital city and around 1.3 million in late 2015 for the second round distribution in the region of Segou.

With FY 2014 funds PMI procured 1.35 million nets that just arrived in May 2015. These nets were originally planned to support the second round mass distribution in the region of Segou, but now they will be used for 2015/2016 routine distribution to pregnant women and infants and the Global Fund will support the mass campaign in Segou.

Commodity gap analysis

Table 2. ITN Gap Analysis

Calendar Year	2015	2016	2017
Total targeted population	17,819,147	18,341,245	18,874,286
Continuous Distribution Needs			
Channel #1: ANC*	890,957	917,062	943,714
Channel #2: EPI **	712,766	733,650	754,971
Estimated Total Need for Continuous	1,603,723	1,650,712	1,698,685
Mass Distribution Needs			
2015 mass distribution campaign (Sikasso, Bamako, and Segou regions)	4,700,000	0	0
2016 mass distribution campaign (Gao, Tombouctou, and Kidal regions)	0	912,895	0
2017 mass distribution campaign (Koulikoro and Kayes regions)	0	0	2,463,000
Estimated Total Need for Campaigns	4,700,000	912,895	2,463,000
Total Calculated Need: Routine and Campaign	**6,303,723**	**2,563,607**	**4,161,685**
Partner Contributions			
ITNs carried over from previous year	2,995,000	1,038,626	1,087,914
ITNs from MoH	0	300,000	300,000
ITNs from Global Fund Round	2,997,349	912,895	0
ITNs from other donors	0	0	0
ITNs planned with PMI funding	1,350,000	1,400,000	1,500,000
Total ITNs Available	**7,342,349**	**3,651,521**	**2,887,914**
Total ITN Surplus (Gap)	**1,038,626**	**1,087,914**	**(1,273,771)**

Population estimates are obtained from the NMCP based on the 2009 census with an estimated 3.6% population growth. Routine nets are given at the first ANC visit for pregnant women and at EPI visits for infants:

*Pregnant women = 5% total population

**Infants = 4% total population.

Plans and justification

PMI will continue to support the nationwide routine distribution through ANC and EPI services while the Global Fund will support the implementation of the phased rolling campaign in the five southern regions plus the capital city Bamako.

Proposed activities with FY 2016 funding: ($6,125,000)

ITN procurement: PMI will procure 1,500,000 ITNs to support the routine distribution to children under one year of age and pregnant women through routine services nationwide. The routine distribution channels, which represent 40% of the overall need in country, will be covered entirely through PMI's procurement plus a portion of the MoH procurement. It is anticipated that the needs for mass campaigns to replace nets distributed in 2014 and prior in Koulikoro and Kayes will be covered by the Global Fund. ($6,002,000)

Distribution of ITNs: PMI will support the distribution of free ITNs through routine ANC and immunization services at the CSCOM level for infants and pregnant women. PMI will also support steps to ensure that ITNs reach the targeted populations (ensure that health workers are distributing ITNs according to national guidance, verifying stocks, and comparing data for nets distributed versus physical stock). These funds will complement distribution funds from other donors and from the GoM. ($123,000)

2. Indoor residual spraying

NMCP/PMI objectives

With PMI support, the NMCP developed a vector control strategy, which proposes that at least 80% of the population is protected by IRS in targeted areas. Since the start of the IRS program in Mali, blanket IRS coverage for targeted districts has been the strategy. As the entire country, except for the extreme northern Sahara regions, is considered high burden, IRS planning is informed by entomology surveillance data.[2] At present, PMI is the only partner supporting the NMCP's IRS strategy. Private mining companies conduct routine spraying campaigns in villages surrounding their mining concessions. Advocacy on the part of the NMCP and PMI may garner support from partners (such as private mining companies expanding their area of operations), and guide future decisions regarding IRS implementation.

Progress since PMI was launched

Historically, IRS in Mali relied on pyrethroid class insecticides. In 2010, in response to evidence of resistance, IRS shifted to using carbamate class products, and eventually, in 2014-2015, to organophosphate class products. PMI has supported spraying in up to three districts as indicated in Table 3. The IRS partnership between the NMCP, PMI, the LBMA (*Laboratoire de Biologie Moléculaire Appliquée*/Laboratory of Applied Molecular Biology, University of Bamako), which supports the monitoring and evaluation of vector control measures, has also benefitted from coordination

---

[2] PMI database. Insecticide decay rate and vector-insecticide resistance data collected at entomology surveillance sites in the IRS target districts.

and shared expertise with LBMA providing biochemical and molecular analysis of collected vectors in order to profile and map vector infection rates and physiological resistance mechanisms. Tables 4 and 5 provide a summary of the entomological monitoring sites and the relevant data that are collected at each site.

Table 3: PMI-supported IRS activities (2013-2017)

Calendar Year	Districts Sprayed	Insecticide class	Structures Sprayed	Coverage Rate[1]	Population Protected
2013	Koulikoro	carbamate	60,150	97%	227,309
	Bla	carbamate	97,174	98%	346,675
	Baroueli	carbamate	71,661	98%	276,120
2014	Koulikoro	carbamate	61,234	98%	223,012
	Bla	organophosphate	96,229	98%	334,115
	Baroueli		70,660	98%	279,441
2015[2]	Koulikoro	organophosphate	61,234	TBD	TBD
	Baroueli		70,660		
2016[3]	Koulikoro	TBD	TBD		
	Baroueli				
	Bla[4]				
2017[3]	Koulikoro				
	Baroueli				
	Bla[4]				

[1] % of structures targeted
[2] based on draft 2015 work plan
[3] IRS districts and insecticides to be informed by surveillance, Mali IRS strategy document (approval pending)
[4] assumes approval of UNITAID grant

Table 4: Mali Resistance monitoring sites and their relevant characteristics

Region	District	Factors considered in selection	Resistance monitoring
Kayes	1. Kita	-Agricultural insecticide use - ITN distribution	- Monitoring of resistance to the four classes of insecticide with WHO susceptibility tube test - Monitoring of resistance intensity to pyrethroids with CDC bottle assay - Characterization of insecticide resistance mechanisms
Koulikoro	2. Koulikoro	-IRS -ITN distribution	
	3. Kati	-ITN distribution / use -Black fly control -Irrigation	
Segou	4. Niono	- Irrigation	
	5. Bla	-Traditional agriculture (limited use of herbicides only) -Sprayed from 2008 to 2014	
	6. Baraoueli	-IRS	
Sikasso	7. Bougouni	-Agricultural insecticide use -ITN distribution	
	8. Silengue	-Irrigation -ITN distribution	
	9. Kadiolo	-Agricultural insecticide use -ITN distribution	
Mopti	10. Badiangara	-Traditional agriculture (limited use of herbicides only)	
	11. Bankass		
	12. Djenne		
District of Bamako	13. Commune IV	-ITN distribution / use	

Table 5: Mali IRS entomological monitoring sites and their relevant characteristics

Region	District	Factors considered in selection	IRS entomological monitoring
Koulikoro	1. Koulikoro	-IRS -ITN distribution	- Density - Behavior - Longevity - EIRs - Blood meal origin
	2. Kati	-ITN distribution / use -Black fly control -Irrigation	
Segou	3. Bla	-Traditional agriculture (limited use of herbicides only) -Sprayed from 2008 to 2014	
	4. Baraoueli	-IRS	
	5. Segou	-Traditional agriculture (limited use of herbicides only)	

Progress during the last 12-18 months

PMI-supported surveillance occurred at 13 sites[3]. Both IRS-targeted and non-IRS sites (selected for reasons such as agriculatural use of insecticides, irrigation, traditional farming without insecticides) were included to inform the question of impact and to monitor indicators such as vector-insecticide resistance and IRS residual effectiveness. The prinicipal malaria vectors, *An. gambaie* s.l. and *An. funestus,* were collected and tested. Highlights include: residual effectiveness of six months after IRS using a long-lasting formulation of an organophosphate (OP) class insecticide, and evidence of complete vector-insecticide susceptibility to OP insecticides, despite the presence of resistance to the pyrethroid-class insecticides in all regions where monitoring occurs.

Both OP and carbamate (CARB) class insecticides were used for IRS in 2014. Entomological monitoring of insecticide decay rates indicated a relatively short residual life of less than two months following IRS with CARB class insecticides in Baraoueli and Bla districts (shorter than the malaria transmission season). Therefore, in 2014, PMI introduced a long-acting OP formulation to ensure adequate protection during the main malaria transmission season. CARB class insecticide was used in Koulikoro District because the insecticide's residual life there was judged to be better based on 2013 monitoring results. Figures 3 and 4 compare the residual effect of each class based on IRS entomological monitoring data collected monthly between July and November 2014. Figures 5 and 6 provide evidence of the impact of OP and CARB class IRS on vector density, including spillover effects into non-spray areas. Additional highlights of the 2014 IRS campaign include:

- structures sprayed: 228,123
- population protected: 836,568
- Post-campaign bioassay testing confirmed correct dosing of insecticide.

---

[3] Mali 2014 End of Spray Report. PMI / Africa IRS (AIRS) Project (IRS2)

Figure 3. Insecticide residual effect following IRS with OP class insecticide (2 districts), 2014.
Observed % mortality following exposure of susceptible malaria vectors to sprayed wall

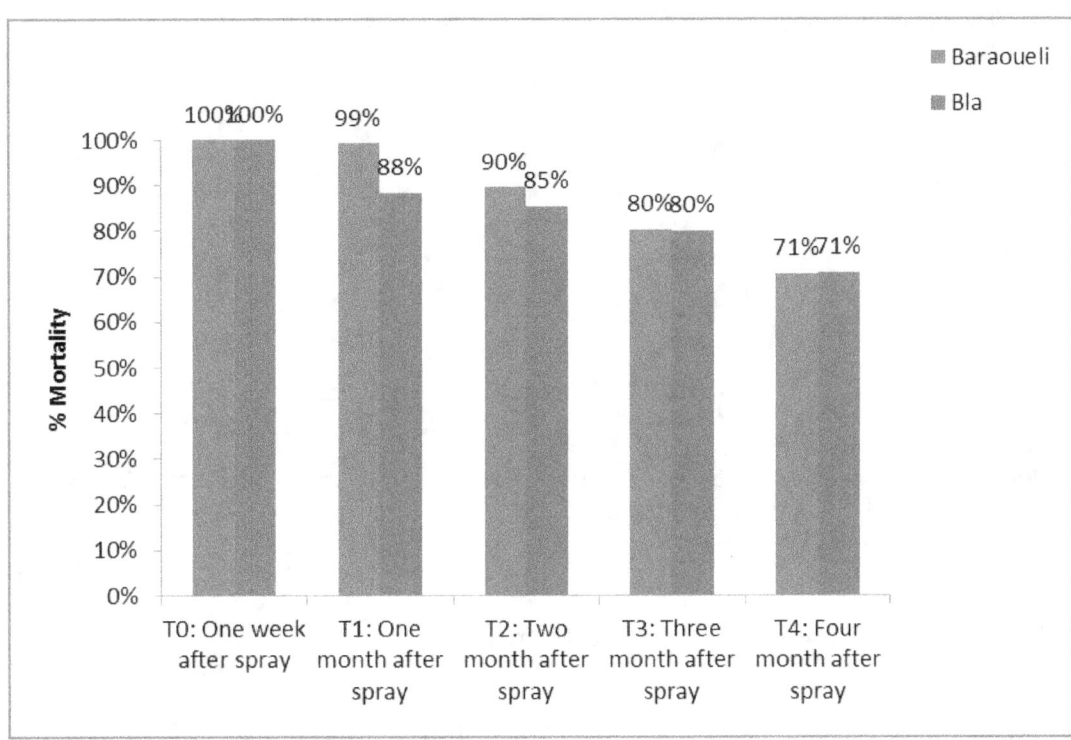

World Health Organization assessment procedure.

Figure 4. Insecticide residual effect following IRS with CARB class insecticide (1 district), 2014.
Observed % mortality following exposure of susceptible malaria vectors to sprayed wall

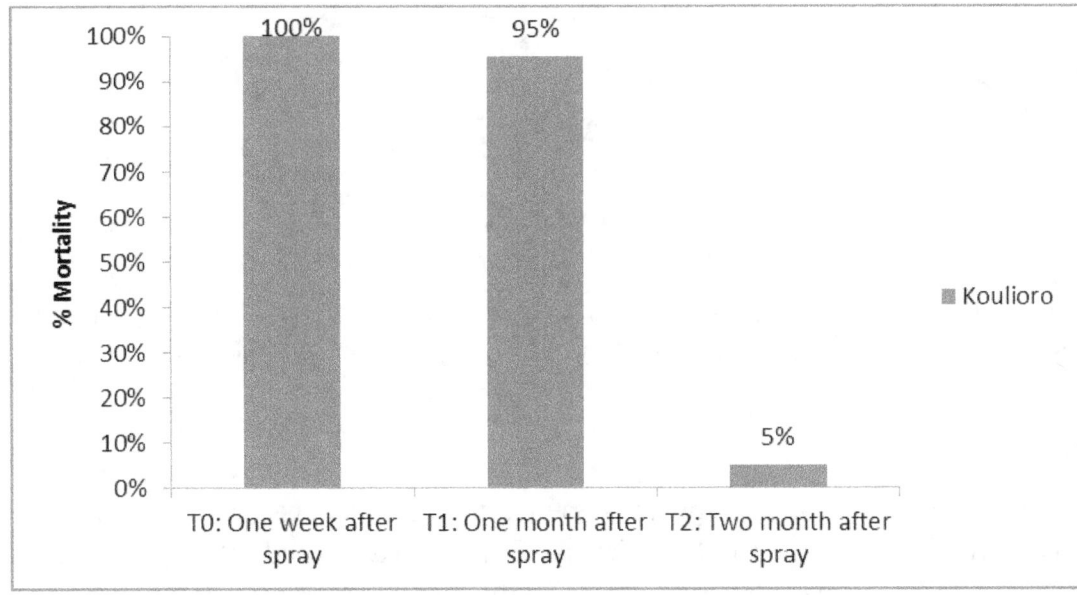

Figure 5. Impact of OP class (pyrimiphos methyl) IRS on vector density

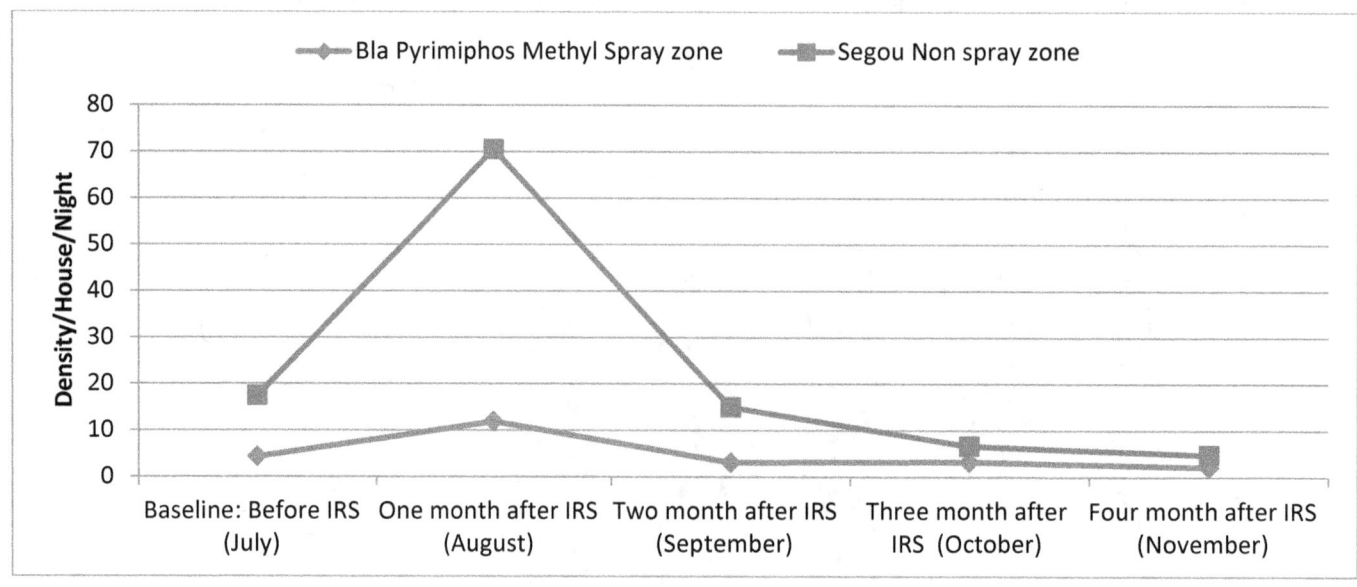

Figure 6. Impact of CARB class (bendiocarb) IRS on vector density

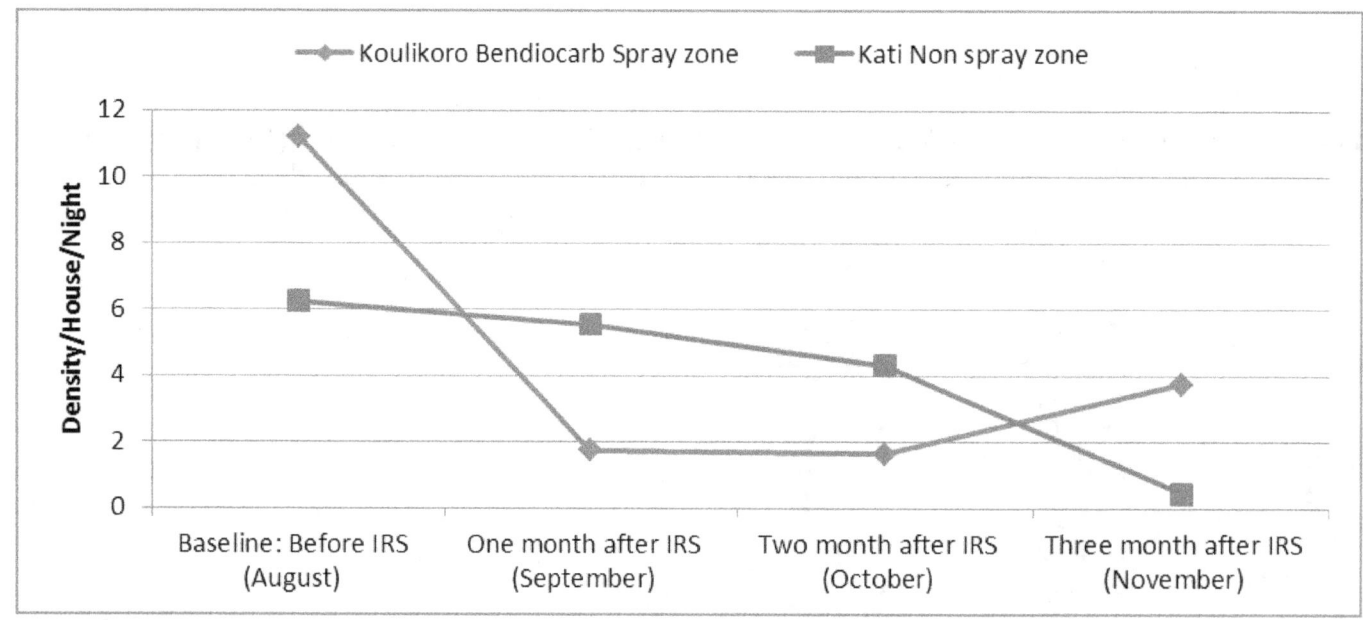

Plans and justification

The 2015 IRS campaign will utilize an organophosphate-class insecticide, which, based on surveillance results, is anticipated to (1) provide protection for the entire transmission season, and (2) be unaffected by existing vector-insecticide resistance mechanisms. Unfortunately, due to higher insecticide costs, implementing this campaign will be more expensive. The 2015 IRS campaign therefore covers a smaller area and two districts (Baroueli and Koulikoro), rather than three districts (Baroueli, Koulikoro and Bla), will be sprayed. Bla will continue to receive the full package of malaria control programming, including complete coverage with ITNs, and will also benefit from the expansion of SMC in the region.

The 'increasing insecticide cost' issue may benefit from a proposal submitted to UNITAID by IVCC, in collaboration with PMI, the Global Fund, and MACEPA to accelerate the uptake of longer-lasting IRS insecticides. Mali was included as one of the proposed countries and is awaiting final details of the award. The objective of the proposal is to subsidize the longer-lasting insecticides (by as much as 35%) to enable countries to use the cost savings to extend implementation. At the time of the MOP writing, Mali had not yet received official word on the award of this grant.

With FY 2016 funds, PMI proposes the continuation of IRS (2017 campaign) in at least two districts, where seasonal transmission patterns and high transmission rates remain a problem. If the UNITAID proposal is approved, the Mali team will organize discussions with PMI's Vector Control group, and the NMCP, to revise PMI's IRS program in Mali. Among the factors to be considered will be the UNITAID subsidized insecticide costs, the overall costs of IRS implementation in Mali, and the National Vector Control Strategy and priorities. The revised IRS plan will be submitted to PMI leadership for approval prior to implementation and any changes in the budget in this MOP will be addressed through the reprogramming process.

Furthermore, political stability and improved epidemiological monitoring (details in the M&E section) will facilitate a wider targeting of IRS to areas of chronic high transmission. PMI will also continue to support entomological monitoring across Mali, to collect data on the standard PMI indicators, as well as information on the physiological basis of insecticide resistance in local vectors, collaboration with the LBMA) at the University of Bamako to better inform selection of IRS insecticides. Finally, there will be renewed emphasis on coordination with and capacity building at the NMCP as well as advocay for expanded IRS, as called for in a new national IRS strategy document.

Proposed activities with FY 2016 funding: ($4,776,083)

Conduct IRS: PMI will support the implementation of IRS using organophosphate in two high burden districts to protect 500,000 people. Procure IRS equipment (insecticide, sprayers, etc.), training, implementation, data collection, protocols, guidelines, BCC, logistic assessment, technical assistance for spraying/entomological assessment. ($4,397,083)

Conduct IRS entomology monitoring and evaluation: Continue to support routine entomological monitoring in 13 sites throughout the country. Support the NMCP entomologist in conducting IRS-related entomological monitoring. Strengthen capacity of DHPS to participate in the monitoring of IRS operations, training of spray operators and to provide coordination with the NMCP on district IRS operations. Mapping insecticide resistance and mosquito biting behavior nationwide. ($300,000)

Procure entomological supplies:. Procure and transport specialized entomological equipment from CDC/Atlanta to Mali for entomological monitoring activities. ($10,000)

Conduct environmental compliance monitoring: Implement a new round of environmental compliance monitoring in two IRS districts (Koulikoro and Baroueli). ($40,000)

Two CDC TDYs: Technical assistance from CDC entomologist for monitoring IRS implentation. ($29,000)

3. Malaria in pregnancy

NMCP/PMI objectives

Mali's malaria in pregnancy (MIP) strategy applies WHO's three-pronged approach: providing three doses of IPTp with SP, promoting the use of ITNs distributed free at the first ANC visit, and effective case management of malarial illness. The NMCP has set ambitious goals for MIP through the National Strategic Plan. The program aims to provide 100% of pregnant women living in stable transmission zones three doses of SP for IPTp at ANC services as per the national guidelines. The NMCP also has a goal of universal coverage with ITNs and, as part of that policy, intends to provide mosquito nets to 100% of pregnant women through ANC clinics, as a supplement to the mass campaign distribution. In 2006, the MoH issued directives ensuring free provision of SP for IPTp (although women do pay a small fee – approximately $1 – for their ANC card). In October 2012, WHO changed its recommendations for IPTp to administering a dose of SP at every ANC visit after quickening. Much of the original research behind this policy change occurred in Mali, so Mali became an early adopter of the new recommendations and revised the national policy in November 2012. Mali is in the process of updating its guidelines for iron and folic acid supplementation. The new guidelines require 0.4 mg or 400 µg (daily) and 60 mg of iron (daily). In case of anemia, 120 mg of iron need to be given until recovery. Once these guidelines are finished they will be distributed to the districts.

Utilization of ANC services by pregnant women is moderate but increasing. In 2001, only 57% of women attended ANC at least once. As of 2012, approximately 74% of women attended ANC at least once during their most recent pregnancy, with 41% making 4+ visits. Urban women access care more frequently than rural women. Two-thirds (67%) of urban women attend ANC four or more times during their pregnancies, as compared to 35% of rural women. At the same time, 25% of women do not attend ANC at all, according to the 2012-2013 DHS. Women in Mali tend to seek antenatal care late in their pregnancies, with the average gestational age for the first ANC consultation being 4.2 months. IPTp use is low, as the 2012-2013 DHS showed that only 20% of women received two doses of SP at ANC visits (up from 4% in the 2006 DHS). Health facilities also collect and report information quarterly through the national HMIS on the number of ANC visits (including early ANC visits), postnatal consultations, SP doses administered, and assisted deliveries by a skilled birth attendant. In 2007, the MoH released revised ANC visit cards that included IPTp and ITN information. The use of bed nets in general is very high in Mali and data from the DHS 2012 show that approximately 73% of pregnant women slept under an ITN the night before the survey.

For case management in pregnancy, the national policy is to use quinine in the first trimester and the first-line ACT (artemether-lumefantrine) (AL) in the second and third trimesters. Treatment of severe malaria follows the same protocols as with non-pregnant adults: injectable artesunate (preferred) and if not available, quinine. Details on PMI's support to the overall case management program, including drug procurement and supply chain management, are available in the case management section of this MOP.

Integration and coordination between the NMCP and the MoH's Reproductive Health Division is critical in ensuring effective MIP programs and high IPTp coverage. Since 2006, the NMCP and the

Reproductive Health Division have developed a revised in-service training module for focused antenatal care (FANC), which includes MIP and IPTp. A MIP working group involving all stakeholders and co-chaired by the NMCP and the reproductive health division has been set up since 2013 and meets regularly to coordinate activities among the stakeholders.

The National Center for Information, Education, and Communication for Health (*Centre National d'Information Education et Communication pour la Santé* - CNIECS), which is tasked with creating BCC materials and strategies, is addressing barriers to increasing uptake of IPTp by improving providers' interpersonal communication skills and encouraging early ANC visits by pregnant women.

Progress since PMI was launched

PMI has been a principal supporter of malaria in pregnancy activities since the beginning of its program in Mali. PMI has supported in-service training and supervision of health providers, in collaboration with the Reproductive Health Division, NMCP, and Midwives Association to facilitate the implementation of the MIP guidelines as well as the training of health providers on interpersonal communication, an area cited by the MoH as a challenge.

PMI has traditionally been the sole procurer of SP for IPTp programs, filling the needs for all pregnant women since the initiative started in Mali. However, beginning in 2016, the MoH will procure limited quantities of SP as well (see Table 6 for details).

To explore the reasons for the low uptake of IPTp in Mali, PMI supported an assessment of the barriers to implementation of IPTp in ANC clinics. The assessment indicated that, in general, women knew about IPTp and had favorable opinions about taking SP to prevent complications of MIP. At the same time, the assessment highlighted a number of misconceptions regarding IPTp on the part of both providers and pregnant women. Among the findings was the pervasive belief that SP cannot be taken on an empty stomach, nor can it be taken after the seventh or eighth month of pregnancy. The most recent policy recommendations from WHO address many of these issues directly, and Mali has retooled their training and supervision materials to address these issues. Although training on the new IPTp recommendations began slowly due to the absence of an implementing partner, there are plans in place with the new partner to ensure that all providers are trained (or retrained if their most recent training is more than two years old) in the new IPTp protocol. In addition, the new DHIS2 system, which is currently being rolled out, will collect data on IPTp3 distribution.

Other PMI-supported partners have promoted the provision of free ITNs to pregnant women at their first ANC visit; in practice, ITNs are often not given until the third or fourth month of pregnancy due to late initiation of ANC. PMI supported a multi-channel BCC strategy targeting pregnant women, women of childbearing age, and men, focusing on knowledge and perceptions related to MIP, women's awareness of risks of malaria during pregnancy, early and frequent ANC attendance at health facility, early use of IPTp in the second trimester, completion of the recommended three treatment courses of IPTp, provision of a free ITN at the first ANC visit, and increasing demand for proper treatment of MIP.

Progress during the last 12-18 months

Mali has had a history of stockouts of SP which have affected the program's ability to deliver services. PMI and its supply chain partners worked to improve procurement and distribution issues. At the central level, efforts were made to ensure sufficient quantities of SP were ordered and delivered in a timely fashion. Within Mali, supply chain partners worked to improve the distribution system down to the CSCOM level (see details in the pharmaceutical management section). The end result was a noticeable improvement in the availability of SP at the CSCOM level. The February 2015 EUV survey showed that 28% of health facilities were stocked out of SP on the day of the survey, down from 85% in 2011. Supply chain issues continue to be a concern and several activities aimed at addressing this issue are included in the pharmaceutical management section of this MOP.

Progress this past year was slowed by the several bilateral projects coming to an end while the new projects had not yet been awarded. Nonetheless, a 'bridge' mechanism allowed some activities to continue and MIP was included in the basic training and service delivery package of activities. A PMI-commissioned study on the national policy documents highlighted several differences in MIP-related guidance between NMCP reference documents and those produced by the Reproductive Health Division. Acting on these findings, PMI and partners produced updated materials to harmonize the guidance documents and bring them in line with new WHO recommendations around IPTp. In addition, during the past year, PMI partners trained 185 health workers on FANC and MIP activities.

Commodity gap analysis

PMI will support the NMCP objective of 100% coverage of all pregnant women by IPTp in accordance with the WHO recommendations. Just before this MOP planning exercise, a Global Fund concept note was submitted which included the procurement of a small quantity of SP for IPTp by the GoM. This gap analysis was based on data from the 2012-2013 DHS regarding ANC utilization patterns, and estimates of the SP quantities included in the Global Fund Concept Note. Mali is also working to increase ANC utilization and, if routine monitoring indicates an increased need for SP, PMI will procure additional doses through reprogramming as needed.

Table 6. SP Gap Analysis for Malaria in Pregnancy

Calendar Year	2015	2016	2017
Total population	17,819,147	18,341,245	18,874,286
SP Needs			
Total number of pregnant women attending ANC*	659,308	687,797	707,786
Total SP Need (in treatments)	**1,977,925**	**2,063,390**	**2,123,357**
Partner Contributions			
SP carried over from previous year	0	0	168,032
SP from MoH	0	231,422	145,086
SP from Global Fund	0	0	0
SP from other donors	0	0	0
SP planned with PMI funding	1,800,000	2,000,000	2,000,000
Total SP Available	1,800,000	2,231,422	2,313,118
Total SP Surplus (Gap)	**(177,925)**	**168,032**	**189,761**

*Assumptions: Approximately 5% of the population could become pregnant. The NMCP bases SP needs on three doses for each pregnant woman attending ANC. The 2012-2013 DHS shows that approximately 75% of pregnant women attend at least one ANC visit during their pregnancies so quantifications are based on that figure.

Plans and justification

PMI will support the NMCP and MoH with its multipronged approach to MIP, including contributing to annual MIP commodity needs (ITNs and SP), improving facility-level FANC services and health provider practices through training and supervision, and promoting coverage of MIP interventions through community mobilization and BCC messages. PMI will support early and frequent attendance of pregnant women at ANCs, and work with the MoH and other donors to ensure SP is available, used correctly, and provided free to pregnant women for IPTp. Through training of health providers in FANC to address barriers to implementation of IPTp and strengthening of the commodity system, PMI will continue to improve MIP services and increase IPTp rates. PMI will also support engagement and mobilization of pregnant women and the promotion of MIP services at the community level through traditional leaders, midwives, and coordinated and harmonized BCC activities. To support innovation in the area of quality of care for ANC, PMI is proposing an operational research study of enhanced training and supervision to improve uptake of IPTp (see OR section for details).

Proposed activities with FY 2016 funding: ($750,000)

SP Procurement: PMI will procure 2 million SP doses to cover the annual need for the estimated 700,000 pregnant women attending ANC in 2017, including handling and distribution costs. ($300,000)

Strengthen FANC and MIP services: PMI will continue to work with the NMCP and partners to improve the FANC and MIP services, including the roll out of the updated MIP guidelines to the regions not already covered. PMI will support training of health providers to provide quality services to pregnant women at ANC visits including ensuring the provision of free SP for IPTp. PMI will work with partners, including the MoH Reproductive Health Division and the Midwives Association, to expand use of the in-service FANC training module and increase supportive supervision during IPTp implementation nationally through facility and community outreach activities. ($450,000)

4. **Case management**

    a) **Diagnosis and Treatment**

NMCP/PMI objectives

Mali's case management policy is in line with WHO guidelines requiring that every malaria case should be laboratory confirmed before administering ACTs and that RDTs should be used to confirm the diagnosis where microscopy is not available. Microscopic diagnosis is performed in 4 national, 6 regional, and 64 district hospitals at a cost ranging from $0.75-$5 per blood smear. In addition to hospitals providing microscopy, some privately operated CSCOMs staffed with physicians and/or laboratory technicians also perform malaria microscopy. However, most CSCOMs do not have the capacity to do microscopy and rely on RDTs for malaria diagnosis. The RDTs initially were free for children under five years of age and pregnant women and highly subsidized for other groups. However, following PMI-supported advocacy by the NMCP, the MoH signed a new policy in mid-2014 to make RDTs free for patients of all ages to encourage RDT use.

The National Institute of Public Health Research *(Institut National de Recherche en Santé Publique* [INRSP]) is responsible for quality control (QC) of all diagnostic services. With PMI funding, the institute has developed and finalized a quality assurance/quality control (QA/QC) plan for malaria microscopy and RDTs. However, implementation of the plan was suspended after the military *coup* in March 2012, but is scheduled to restart in 2015.

In 2010, the MoH revised the national policy for the treatment of uncomplicated malaria to make artemether-lumefantrine (AL) the first-line drug and artesunate-amodiaquine (AS/AQ) as an alternative. As per national directive, ACTs are free to children under five years of age and pregnant women in the second and third trimester. Mali's malaria case management guidelines were recently updated to specify injectable artesunate as the first-line treatment for severe malaria, with intravenous quinine and injectable artemether as alternatives. In practice, however, health centers typically use whatever severe malaria medication is available. In addition, the People's Pharmacy of Mali (PPM) has a significant stock of quinine, so both will be used in 2015 and 2016 as injectable artesunate is being scaled up, and the availability and use of quinine diminishes.

Progress since PMI was launched

Since 2008, PMI has contributed to the improvement of malaria diagnosis and clinical case management in Mali by providing support to local NGOs and partners to conduct a combination of various strengthening activities for health workers, laboratory technicians, and community health workers. These activities include trainings of trainers, refresher training courses and supervision of malaria microscopy and RDTs, adherence to test results when prescribing ACTs and improvement of care for patients with severe febrile disease.

The NMCP and MRTC initiated supervision of diagnosis and treatment for malaria cases in 2010 starting with Bamako and transitioning to other regions. These visits covered district referral health centers (CSREFs), where the team provided training of trainers to district health leads to provide supervisory support in their specific district. The team used supervisory tools developed in collaboration with NMCP, PMI, MRTC, and malaria partners to focus on the proportion of suspected malaria cases tested, adherence to malaria diagnostic test results, and improving case management of severe febrile disease. Malaria supervision guidelines were updated in February 2012 and include supervision of outpatient consultations at health facilities, antenatal consultations, and ASC visits.

Diagnostic confirmation of all suspected malaria cases has increased substantially in the last five years: routine data show that 18% of suspected malaria cases were tested by microscopy or RDT in 2010, increasing to 32% in 2011, 52% in 2012, and 80% in 2013. According to the 2014 annual NMCP report, health workers diagnostically tested 90% of suspected malaria cases prior to treatment.

A PMI-supported national health facility assessment in 2012 found that about half of suspected malaria cases were diagnostically confirmed: 63% of children under five with suspected malaria were tested with either microscopy or RDT, while 47% of over-five patients with suspected malaria were tested at these facilities. The survey found good availability of ACTs at health facilities, with 92% of facilities surveyed having ACTs in stock. However, the assessment showed poor performance of health workers on treatment of severe malaria, and problematic routine data given an implausibly high percentage of severe malaria cases diagnosed.

Training and supervision of health workers at facilities have been slow in the last few years due to temporary suspension of activities after a military *coup* in March 2012 and a gap in PMI case management activities at the health facility due to a lag between implementing programs close-out and start-up. The Global Fund committed to funding malaria case management refresher training of health workers nationwide, with trainings completed at the national and regional levels and ongoing training at the health district level.

Poor access to care – due to geographic and economic constraints – is a major challenge for malaria treatment in Mali. With approximately 1,206 CSCOMs in the country in 2013, about 90% of the population has geographic access to public health services according to WHO standards (living within 15 km of a first-line health facility) but only 57% live within 5 km of a health facility. All patients must pay consultation fees, however diagnosis by RDT is free for all as of 2014, and ACTs are free for children under five. Older patients must pay fees for malaria drugs, though these are subsidized. A health financing task force has been set up to examine issues related to user fees for primary care in Mali, a complex issue with a long history dating back to the Bamako Initiative in 1987 that set up revolving drug funds at CSCOMs. An updated national health financing policy and strategy was adopted in February 2014, which outlines a strategy to increase the proportion of the population covered by insurance from 6% in 2011 to 45% in 2023, primarily through expanding *mutuelle* insurance for the informal sector.

To overcome geographic barriers to health services, the MoH adopted an integrated community case management (iCCM) package in February 2010 that includes treatment for malaria, diarrhea, pneumonia, and malnutrition; essential newborn care; and family planning. Free malaria treatment for children under five is provided by trained ASCs (though patients must pay a consultation fee) and includes malaria diagnosis with RDTs and treatment with ACTs, although diarrhea and pneumonia medications are not free. Severe cases are referred to CSCOMs. ASCs are paid a salary of approximately $100 per month, with various donors currently supporting ASC salaries in different regions. One of the NMCP's major concerns is securing continued funding for ASC salaries. From 2016 – 2018, the Global Fund committed to paying approximately 60% (1,500 ASCs out of 2,317 currently trained) of the salary costs of the iCCM program through its agreement with the government of Mali. In addition, the GoM is also revising its community strategy (called 'SEC' locally), to reduce donor costs and to incorporate cost recovery into the program with a goal of sustainability over the long term. PMI and other USAID health funds (MCH, Nutrition/WASH, FP) will support the implementation of iCCM in all 20 districts of the regions of Kayes and Sikasso. The Global Fund, UNICEF, World Vision, and other partners will support iCCM activities in the regions of Koulikoro, Ségou, and Mopti, where an iCCM technical group coordinates all partners' interventions.

Mali currently has 2,317 trained ASCs who are functional in five of the eight regions of the country in the south, where more than 90% of the population lives. However, there is a need for additional ASCs and roughly 2,600 ASC posts are currently unfilled. According to the NMCP's preliminary 2014 annual report, a total of 233,837 suspected malaria cases were tested by ASCs and 181,103 cases confirmed positive, although 184,340 were treated with ACTs. The ASCs work in collaboration with volunteer *relais*, community members who assist in community mobilization and behavior change communication. An external evaluation completed in May 2014 found that iCCM was well integrated into the health system of Mali and effectively coordinated by partners, although utilization was still low, due in part to financial barriers. PMI is working with other stakeholders to coordinate and expand iCCM/SEC activities although the three regions of the North are still not accessible due to security concerns.

The total population of PMI's target regions for iCCM (Koulikoro, Sikasso, Bamako, and Kayes) in 2017 is projected to be 6,526,298, of which 2,055,493 will be children under five (the targeted group for iCCM). In 2017, PMI will contribute to the scale-up to cover all districts in USAID-targeted regions through the Mission's integrated program with financial support from other health programs including Maternal and Child Heath, Family Planning and nutrition/water, sanitation, and hygiene.

In the 2013–2017 Malaria Strategic Plan, Mali introduced SMC (providing four rounds of SP and AS/AQ for children under five years of age) as a key malaria control intervention. SMC is implemented by the district health team which distributes the medications at a fixed point (often near the CSCOM each month). Participation of the ASCs varies by district including conducting BCC activities, and going door-to-door to recruit families who do not come to the central distribution point. Following a successful pilot of SMC in Koutiala District (in the Sikasso Region) by MSF in 2012, which showed a 42% reduction in malaria cases, the NMCP developed a plan to implement SMC in all districts of Mali, with scale-up dependent upon donor funds. In 2013, five of Mali's 64 districts were covered by SMC and increased to 21 districts during the 2014 transmission season, including one supported by PMI. Due to a three-year grant awarded to CRS from UNITAID, SMC will be implemented in at least 42 districts during the 2015 transmission season. PMI currently supports the implementation SMC in four districts in the regions of Kayes and Sikasso. To the existing PMI-supported districts, six new districts (to be selected in 2016) from the regions of Sikasso and Kayes will be added. SMC will be implemented in the iCCM districts and by 2017 all the districts will be covered with both interventions. The iCCM is implemented by the ASCs and SMC by both ASCs and community volunteers (*relais*). The same ASCs involved in the year-round iCCM implementation will handle SMC drug distribution during SMC implementation. Of the 42 districts, PMI will support the implementation in 10 districts in the focus regions of Kayes, Koulikoro, and Sikasso.

During the 2015 transmission season, PMI will support a therapeutic efficacy study (TES) of first (AL) and second-line (AS/AQ) ACTs in the high malaria burden rural communes of Kolokani (region of Koulikoro) and Selingue (region of Sikasso). Children six months to five years of age with uncomplicated *Plasmodium falciparum* malaria will be randomized to receive either treatment. A total of 120 children will be selected for each study arm. In addition to RDT confirmation and randomized ACT treatment, thick and thin blood smears will be prepared for each participant on days 0, 2, 3, 7, 14, 21, 28, 35, and 42 to assess asexual parasitemia and response to treatment. Parasite positive samples will be preserved on filter paper for subsequent genotyping to discriminate between new infection and recurrent parasites using molecular K13 markers at the Centers for Disease Control and Prevention (CDC) (see M&E section for funding details)

Progress during the last 12-18 months

Since PMI's bilateral service delivery implementing partner finished operations in September 2013 and there was no implementing partner for most of FY 2014, only limited PMI-funded case management activities took place from September 2013 to September 2014. A new implementing partner began in December 2014, and will focus on improving quality of malaria diagnostics and clinical case management. The partner will work in partnership with the *Institut National de Recherche en Santé Publique* (INRSP) to build and strengthen capacity of a cohort of staff with known competencies to train, supervise and mentor laboratory technicians in accurate diagnosis of malaria. The primary goal is to have the cohort of INRSP staff support the NMCP to train, supervise, and mentor diagnostics experts in the four target intervention regions (Kayes, Sikasso, Koulikoro, Bamako), creating synergies with Global Fund interventions. With the widespread use of RDTs in both health facilities and the community, PMI continued support of training and supervision of health facility providers and ASCs on

RDT use and interpretation. Additionally, plans are underway to reinvigorate Outreach Training and Support Supervision (OTSS), which is a quality assurance mechanism proven to be effective, to ensure that training directly contributes to improved quality of malaria diagnostics in the field.

With reprogrammed FY 2014 funding, PMI procured 2,000,000 RDTs for use at health facilities and for ASCs who test febrile children under five in the community. Despite PMI's inability to support RDT training for health workers in 2014, the most recent end-use verification (EUV) survey conducted at 86 facilities in 5 regions throughout Mali in February-March 2015 found that 81% of health workers were trained in RDTs and 84% of laboratory technicians had been trained in microscopy. At the time of the survey, 75% of health facilities had RDTs in stock, and 32% had a stockout of more than three days in the last three months. However, the February-March 2015 EUV survey found that 24% of health facilities surveyed had appropriate stock of RDTs (according to established maximum/minimum policies). With the removal of fees for RDTs for all age groups, the percent of malaria cases that are diagnostically confirmed is anticipated to further increase.

During the last 12–18 months, PMI procured 2.2 million AL for health facilities, iCCM and pregnant women. Based on requests from the NMCP and estimates from the HMIS of 600,000 severe malaria cases per year, PMI procured 125,000 treatments of injectable artesunate. PMI has been supporting iCCM implementation, including initial and refresher trainings and regular supervision, in all districts of Kayes, Koulikoro, Sikasso, and Bamako regions. However, due to the gap of an implementing partner to conduct case management strengthening activities, very few ASCs were trained in 2014 as compared to the 426 trained in 2013. From May 2013–April 2014, ASCs treated approximately 43,267 children with malaria. According to a recent assessment conducted in four PMI-supported districts, caregivers cited financial barriers as a primary deterrent to using ASCs. As a result, ASCs in PMI focus areas reduced consultation prices, which are used to fund community oversight committees, from 300 CFA (~ $0.62) to 100 CFA.

The February-March 2015 EUV survey found that 95% of health facilities had at least one presentation of AL on the day of the visit. However, stockouts for three or more consecutive days within the last three months ranged from 30-46% depending on the presentation. The EUV survey also found that 91% of children under five years of age with malaria were treated with an ACT.

In 2014, PMI funded the implementation and evaluation of the effectiveness of SMC (which included coverage, adherence, cost implications, and impact on parasitemia, morbidity, and drug resistance) in the district of Kita in the Kayes Region, in approximately 100,000 eligible children ages 3–59 months. Preliminary results for year one are outlined in the operational research section. With FY 2015 funding, PMI will support the scale-up of SMC to ten districts in the regions of Kayes, Koulikoro, Sikasso, and Bamako in coordination with other donors.

Commodity gap analysis

At the time of the MOP planning exercise, the NMCP had just submitted their Global Fund concept note to support malaria interventions from January 2016-December 2018. All procurement activities, quantification and consumption data were reviewed to determine PMI's commodity contribution for FY 2016. As part of the MOP process, quantification data for FY 2015 was re-examined to address any immediate gaps. In 2015, the Global Fund procured RDTs of a different brand than currently used in Mali. To avoid the need for nationwide retraining, the NMCP and partners have agreed that Global Fund RDTs will be used to cover the needs for the Sikasso Region only, the most populated region of Mali. PMI will cover gaps in the rest of the country. To meet this challenge, PMI reprogrammed FY 2015 funds to procure an additional 1,000,000 RDTs.

There are no anticipated RDT gaps for FY 2016. PMI has committed to procuring all of the RDTs, while the Global Fund will cover the country's ACT gap. However, the exact amount of the Global Fund's commitment was unknown at the time of MOP planning, so PMI programmed stock of 500,000 AL presentations for routine distribution at the health facilities to ensure availability of ACTs. PMI will monitor donor contributions throughout the year, factoring in consumption data, and make any necessary adjustments to ensure commodity gaps are filled.

The gap analysis does not include quantification of drugs for severe malaria or SMC. The number of cases of severe malaria reported in the SLIS in 2014 was 799,848. However, these cases were not systematically confirmed with malaria diagnostics and likely represent an overestimate of the true number of cases of severe malaria.

Table 7: RDT Gap Analysis

Calendar Year	2015	2016	2017
RDT Needs			
Target population at risk for malaria[1]	17,819,147	18,341,245	18,874286
Total number projected fever cases[2]	11,038,799	11,362,234	11,692,448
Percent of fever cases confirmed with microscopy	18%	18%	18%
Percent of fever cases confirmed with RDT	82%	82%	82%
Total RDT Needs[3]	**2,892,721**	**3,138,880**	**3,570,669**
Partner Contributions			
RDTs carried over from previous year	1,259,647	2,131,251[5]	2,192,371
RDTs from MoH	0	0	0
RDTs from Global Fund	1,764,325	0	0
RDTs from other donors	0	0	0
RDTs planned with PMI funding	2,000,000[4]	3,200,000[6]	3,000,000
Total RDTs Available	**5,023,972**	**5,331,251**	**5,192,371**
Total RDT Surplus (Gap)[7]	**2,131,251**	**2,192,371**	**1,621,702**

Footnotes: [1]100% of the population is the target population at risk for malaria. [2]Total number of projected fever cases at the health facility and community level according to the number of fever cases per person, per year. These figures are derived from the March 2015 SIAPS quantification exercise. [3]Total RDT needs for health facilities and iCCM are based on gap analysis exercise led by NMCP for the development of the Global Fund concept note. [4]This amount includes the original 500,000 listed in the FY 2014 MOP plus the reprogramming request of 1,500,000. [5]There was a large carry-over of Global Fund RDTs, however they were used in the Sikasso Region. [6]This includes the 2 million listed in FY 2015 MOP plus the reprogramming request of 1,200,000. [7]Surplus will vary depending on usage in SMC sites. Procurements may be modified as actual usage figures are known.

Table 8: ACT Gap Analysis

Calendar Year	2015	2016	2017
ACT Needs			
Target population at risk for malaria[1]	17,819,147	18,341,245	18,874,286
Total projected number of malaria cases[2]	1,639,759	1,630,152	1,599,952
Total ACT Needs[3]	**2,219,533**	**2,134,439**	**2,428,055**
Partner Contributions			
ACTs carried over (deficit) from previous year	338,484	1,506,923	2,053,496
ACTs from MoH	0	0	0
ACTs from Global Fund	1,187,972	1,181,012	1,159,132
ACTs from Other Donors	0	0	0
ACTs planned with PMI funding	2,200,000	1,500,000	500,000[4]
Total ACTs Available	**3,726,456**	**4,187,935**	**3,712,628**
Total ACT Surplus (Gap)[5]	**1,506,923**	**2,053,496**	**1,284,573**

Footnotes: [1]100% of the population is the target population at risk for malaria. [2]Total projected number of malaria cases is estimated from 2014 routine malaria data as listed in the gap analysis exercise led by NMCP for the development of the Global Fund concept note. [3]Total ACT needs for health facilities and iCCM are based on gap analysis exercise led by NMCP for the development of the Global Fund concept note. Estimates are adjusted to account for population growth and 100% coverage. [4]The Global Fund committed to procuring the entire ACT needs for calendar year 2017, however, at the time of writing the MOP, the exact amount to be committed was unknown. PMI programmed a buffer stock of 500,000 for health facility distribution. [5]Surplus will vary depending on usage in SMC sites. Procurements may be modified as actual usage figures are known.

Plans and justification

To support the NMCP and sustain the trend of increasing malaria diagnostic confirmation, PMI will procure 3 million RDTs, filling the entire commodity gap in FY 2016. The RDTs will contribute to the needs at the health facility level and iCCM during the 2016-2017 calendar year period.

Global Fund has agreed to procure the majority of the ACT needs, fulfilling the country's AL gap in the public sector. However, at the time of writing the MOP, the exact amount to be purchased was not clear. PMI will procure 500,000 AL as buffer stock, in the event Global Fund is unable to fill the gap. It is important to note that USAID/Mali has identified four priority regions (Koulikoro, Sikasso, Bamako, Kayes) for interventions, however, the PMI program has a national scope so commodities purchased through PMI can be used in any region of Mali where there is need. PMI will also contribute to the procurement of 3,200,000 treatments of SP-AQ co-blister to help fill the treatment gap during the SMC campaign to cover 800,000 children under five for four rounds in ten districts.

For both RDTs and ACTs, current quantifications do not take into account the increased needs at the outset of SMC interventions, when all febrile children are tested and treated if found to have malaria. The estimated surplus of commodities, due to the new Global Fund procurements, will be used to cover these needs. Data on actual RDT and ACT needs during SMC campaigns will be collected and used to adjust the procurements as necessary. PMI will revisit the quantifications during the reprogramming exercise to ensure that procurements more closely reflect actual consumption needs.

Mali is transitioning from using quinine to injectable artesunate for severe malaria. For 2017, there are estimated to be 1.6 million malaria cases, of which approximately 10% could become severe. Given the existing large supply of injectable artesunate currently at the central medical warehouse, and the concurrent use of existing quinine until supplies are used up, PMI will cover roughly 6% of the national need and procure enough doses to cover 96,000 severe malaria cases. PMI will continue to provide support for refresher training and supervision on malaria case management at the health facility level, continuing support initiated with FY 2015 funds.

PMI will continue to support implementation of SMC in 10 districts in four focus regions, covering an estimated 800,000 children with four rounds of treatment with SP-AQ during the high-transmission season. PMI funding will cover the purchase of SMC drugs as well as implementation. Additional funding has been set aside in the M&E section for the expansion of resistance monitoring of SP. PMI will continue to support implementation of the full package of iCCM in the four focus regions of Koulikoro, Sikasso, Bamako, and Kayes.

Proposed activities with FY 2016 funding: ($8,486,000)

Procurement of RDTs: PMI will procure 3,000,000 RDTS to contribute to the RDT needs at CSCOMs and to supply ASCs as part of the national iCCM strategy. ($1,550,000)

Procurement of ACTs: PMI will procure 500,000 treatments of AL for the public sector and 360,000 treatments of SP-AQ for the SMC campaign in non-PMI focus districts. ($1,360,000)

Treatment for severe malaria: PMI will procure 96,000 treatments of injectable artesunate for treatment of patients with severe malaria at CSREF (and selected CSCOM) levels. The estimated annual need is more than 700,000 cases, according to routine reporting, but this is likely a large overestimate given over-diagnosis of severe malaria in Mali. ($420,000)

Distribution of case management commodities: PMI will support the distribution of RDTs, ACTs, SP, and other malaria commodity needs to the district level. ($250,000)

Training and supervision for malaria case management in four regions: After training health personnel at all levels in case management, PMI will continue to support the NMCP to conduct quarterly supervisory visits in order to maintain and strengthen the quality of services at multiple levels of the health delivery system. Particular emphasis will be placed on training and supervision for severe malaria case management. PMI will support improved and increased malaria diagnosis and case management in collaboration with the NMCP at national, regional, district and community levels. This activity will focus on the four USAID priority regions (Koulikoro, Sikasso, Bamako, Kayes). ($600,000)

Training and supervision for malaria case management in Mopti and Segou: PMI will support training on diagnostics, case management for uncomplicated and severe malaria, and supervision on all aspects of case management in two high burden areas not covered by USAID bilateral activities. ($500,000)

Procurement of SMC treatments: PMI will support the cost of covering 800,000 children under five years of age with four rounds of SP-AQ co-blister for SMC. ($1,696,000)

Implementation of SMC: PMI will support the implementation of SMC in 10 districts. Implementation will include the costs of training, supervision, community mobilization, and distribution of drugs. ($1,500,000)

Implementation of iCCM: PMI will support iCCM implementation in the districts of Sikasso, Kayes, Koulikoro, and Bamako, while other donors, including UNICEF, the Global Fund, and the GoM, will provide support for iCCM activities in the other target regions. PMI support for iCCM includes continued support to the malaria/fever component of the iCCM package, with new and refresher trainings at district levels, supportive supervision, training in appropriate RDT use, evaluating ASC performance with RDTs, monitoring and evaluation, and provision of ASC materials and supplies. PMI will support ASCs to provide appropriate health communications and BCC messages to encourage understanding and adherence to current treatment algorithms. PMI will continue to support the NMCP to coordinate all community health implementing partners to ensure that community health materials (e.g., training modules, job aids, supervision protocols, and key messages) are reviewed and standardized across partners. ($600,000)

CDC TDY: PMI will support the cost of one technical assistance visit from a subject matter expert to provide guidance on the quality assurance of diagnostics. ($10,000)

b) **Pharmaceutical Management**

The supply chain system is a combination of push and pull as the central level pushes down to the regions, the community health center staff pulls health commodities from the district pharmacies, and ASCs obtain their health commodities from the community health centers (CSCOMs). Although the districts are responsible for collecting commodities from the regional level, PMI has asked PPM to deliver directly to the districts for immediate supply at lower levels. The regions order monthly from the central level, whereas hospitals are on an automatic system of quarterly ordering. The district pharmacies purchase drugs from regional depots based upon monthly orders from health facilities (CSREFs and CSCOMs) and on the average number of drugs expected to be distributed within the district's catchment area. The PPM distributes malaria commodities per the distribution plan developed by the NMCP with the assistance of partners.

If a drug is unavailable in the regional PPM stores, private pharmaceutical warehouses can fill orders. Ideally, the CSCOMs keep one month of buffer stock and the district drug depot (*dépôt répartiteur des cercles*) keep minimum two months and maximum four months of stock. However, there are problems with drug storage at district depots related to storage capacity, humidity, security, and drug classification in warehouses. While CSCOMs must collect all required drugs from the district pharmaceutical depots, there is no central funding to support the transportation and logistics and often the districts are stocked out or waiting for their request to be filled. The pull portion of the system still proves to be a hurdle, and commodities often do not reach the lowest levels of the health system.

Multiple problems still hamper the Malian supply chain system and the ability to maintain adequate supply. Although interaction among the different levels (national, region, district, and community) has improved, there is still a strong need for better data and communication informing the district and community levels of the arrival of commodities at the regional and district level. At the CSCOM level, there is limited funding to pay and capability for transportation to pick up needed commodities, leading to stockouts, even when there is available stock in country. More accurate forecasting, supply and distribution planning remains an area for improvement as well. Finally, the Bamako Initiative has created a governance issue that directly affects the provision of malaria commodities by creating disincentives. Pregnant women and children under five are supposed to receive ACTs for free under the Bamako Initiative; however adult medicines and other malaria medicines require payment to create a profit that is intended to support the supply chain system. Unfortunately, this has led to a disincentive for providers to order or offer free medicines as there is no financial gain. The negative incentive to request or prescribe free drugs has led to real and artificial stockouts. The MoH and partners continue to raise their concern around the financial incentives issue to find a way to address the unintended consequences. A study is planned to evaluate the economics and effects on provider behavior as a result of the cost recovery system (*please refer to the OR section*).

Regulation and drug quality: Several ministerial decrees provide guidelines for the management of pharmaceuticals in Mali. These include the formation of a national committee to oversee pharmacy retailers responsible for QC, inspection, and licensure and ensuring a basic package of pharmaceutical products. Adherence to standard operating procedures for pharmaceutical management is still a weakness, particularly at the lower levels of the health system. The National Essential Drug List is reviewed biannually. Laws are in place to ensure QC for imported drugs. The Directorate of Drugs and Pharmacies (*Direction de la Pharmacie et du Médicament* [DPM]) issues visas and imports licenses only after the exporter meets certification and other requirements. The National Health Laboratory (*Laboratoire National de la Santé [LNS]*) samples drugs, verifies quality, and has regulatory authority to monitor pre- and post-market quality of drugs and other products, including insecticides and bed nets. The LNS checks the quality of all commodities that arrive at the PPM. Expired or poor quality medicines are destroyed at the national level, however there is no adequate incinerator and medicines are still burned out in the open, but far from populations. The DPM, the National Health Laboratory, and customs officials meet quarterly to discuss regulations and importation or donation of medicines.

Pharmacovigilance: Pharmacovigilance remains a priority of the NMCP and the MoH. The Pharmacovigilance Department at the DPM has developed an action plan, adverse events notification form, and timetable, however the plan needs to be enforced.

NMCP/PMI objectives

A main component of the National Malaria Strategy (2013-2017) is to reach universal coverage of key malaria commodities which cannot be achieved without consistent access and availability of essential malaria commodities through a functioning supply chain system. The NMCP and PMI plan to increase the availability of malaria commodities through a strengthened supply chain system and improved understanding and implementation of logistics and pharmaceutical management tools.

Progress since PMI was launched

The People's Pharmacy of Mali (*Pharmacie Populaire du Mali* [PPM]) manages, procures, and distributes medicines for Mali's primary health care system. The PPM has five regional warehouses in the regions of Kayes, Koulikoro, Sikasso, Segou, and Mopti and three offices in Koutiala, Tombouctou, and Gao. Services from the warehouses at Gao and Tombouctou were disrupted due to the political insecurity but should be functioning again soon and serving their respective regions. PPM delivers all commodities from the central level to the regional level but does not have the capacity to ensure reliable transportation of commodities to the community level. The PPM stores and distributes commodities procured by the GoM and key donors like PMI and the Global Fund. Warehousing for the multitude of commodities is inadequate but plans are underway to increase storage capacity.

Despite a *coup* and disruptions in funding availability from the Global Fund the pharmaceutical management, logistics and quality assurance system has shown improvement since PMI began supporting Mali in 2008. Due to an agreement with the PPM and increased trainings and supervision, commodities now flow past the regional level. There are fewer stockouts as forecasting and distribution plans, logistics management skills, and communications have improved. Availability and use of RDTs and SP for IPTp have also increased as new policy has rolled out. The national laboratory is able to test and report on the quality of malaria pharmaceuticals. Regular coordination meetings now occur among malaria partners regarding commodities and policies in order to make informed commodity and supply chain decisions.

Progress during the last 12-18 months

During the past year PMI continued to provide a significant portion of malaria commodities in concert with the resurgence of Global Fund commodities (*please refer to quantities listed above in case management section*). PMI continues to support the PPM to improve distribution of malaria commodities to the district level. Due to a USAID-supported assessment of the PPM and development of a long term improvement plan, with the majority of activities supported by UNFPA, donors are now underway to ensure better warehousing at the central and regional level (racks, temperature control, classifying systems, cleanliness, training of staff, etc.). The national technical coordination committee continues to meet quarterly to make supply chain decisions. The EUV survey highlighted continued weaknesses in the supply chain system and pharmaceutical management capacity as stockouts, overstocks, poor reporting, and lack of training in pharmaceutical management remain challenges. However, distribution plans are now developed more efficiently between the PPM and NMCP resulting in smoother distribution of commodities once they are received and cleared through the PPM. Efforts to improve logistics reporting, commodity management, data analysis, and pharmaceutical management continues at the regional and district level through quarterly visits, supervision and trainings. PMI and other USAID health elements supported an assessment of the private sector pharmacies in Mali to have a better understanding of the availability and use of ACTs and RDTs and develop recommendations for any potential interventions in the private sector. One recommendation included a request that the MoH provide ACTs and RDTs to the private sector.

In 2014, USAID Mali and PMI supported the PPM to develop an ambitious five-year strategic plan that envisions the building of new warehouse facilities to improve the storage capacity.

Although there have been improvements, there are still persistent problems plaguing the Malian supply chain system and management of pharmaceuticals. Data quality and analysis is poor, storage guidelines, although available, are still not regularly followed, and proper storage amenities or capacity is lacking at most levels. Distribution beyond the regional level is still a challenge due to poor data, communication, and lack of transportation.

Plans and justification

PMI will continue to strengthen supply chain, logistics, and pharmaceutical management including forecasting, quantification, training, supervision and monitoring stocks and malaria commodity needs/gaps. PMI will work with the NMCP, MoH, and appropriate partners for improved supply and distribution plans to ensure that essential life-saving drugs, including ACTs and RDTs, reach the end user. Support to the PPM in delivering malaria drugs and commodities to the regional and district depots will continue. PMI will continue to support the coordinating committee led by the DPM with the participation of the NMCP, PPM, and supply chain partners to improve the quantification and distribution of malaria commodities. PMI will also contribute to strengthening the LMIS system for better data availability and use for decisions making and improve warehousing at the district level. PMI will support the MiniLab® (MQM) sites as part of a longer term strategy for drug quality assurance.

The GoM has a testing and alert system for routine testing of pharmaceutical products available in the health sector followed by regulatory actions when falsified and substandard medicines are found. This system has been challenging due to lack of clarity on who needs to take action and what the correct response should be. PMI will facilitate reviving a committee on counterfeit drugs that has existed but remained inactive due to a lack of resources. The committee will advocate taking regulatory action on substandard and counterfeit medicines found as a result of postmarketing surveillance activities. In parallel, PMI will provide support to the Drug Regulatory Direction of the MoH for conducting follow-up investigations on falsified and substandard antimalarial medicines. PMI will also facilitate defining short term and long term strategies to deal with falsified and substandard medicines including withdrawal and preventive measures. Both the National Laboratory of Health and the Drug Regulatory Direction of MoH are responsible for running the alert system. The Laboratory does the testing/quality control activities while the Drug Regulatory Direction will work on investigations and response. PMI support will be time-limited (1-2 years) to provide the interim support while these institutions organize the activities.

Proposed activities with FY 2016 funding: ($800,000)

Supply chain and logistics strengthening: PMI will continue to provide technical assistance for pharmaceutical management, including forecasting commodity needs; and improved coordination between the NMCP and PPM, through organizations such as the national medicines body. Pharmaceutical and supply chain strengthening activities will include training and supervision in pharmaceutical management, national guidelines, standard operating procedures, quantification and monitoring availability of key antimalarial commodities at the national, district, facility, and community levels. ($500,000)

End-use verification survey: PMI will conduct two EUV surveys to track essential commodities at the health facility level. ($100,000)

Quality assurance and quality control of antimalarials: Strengthen capacity in quality assurance and quality control of antimalarials via increased training at the National Laboratory of Health, supporting the implementation of the five-year strategic plan, supervision of MQM sites. Support will also be provided to the Drug Regulatory Direction of the MoH to improve the alert and response system around counterfeit and substandard medicines. ($200,000)

5. Health system strengthening and capacity building

PMI supports a broad array of health system strengthening activities which cut across intervention areas, such as training of health workers, supply chain management and health information systems strengthening, drug quality monitoring, and NCMP capacity building.

NMCP/PMI objectives

The NMCP objectives for health system strengthening include expanding their ability to train and supervise providers in the field, improving the quality of information available to the NMCP for program management and reporting, and improving the physical working conditions at the NMCP office in Bamako.

Progress since PMI was launched

Through its partners, PMI has worked to strengthen the health surveillance system, the supply chain and pharmaceutical management system, and the capacity of the national laboratory. PMI and partners have also worked to improve the ability of health workers to manage and treat malaria at all levels with a particular focus at the community level. The coordination of malaria program activities across multiple partners has improved in the last few years as evidenced by the successful implementation of the complex new SMC intervention.

PMI supported the evaluation of the HMIS at the national and community levels and continues to work with the HMIS Division of the MoH and other donors to develop a new HMIS based on DHIS 2. Since its launch in Mali, PMI is working with the MoH and partners to improve the coverage of health interventions through the development and implementation of new strategies including iCCM and SMC. PMI also developed the dashboard to capture, track, aggregate, and disseminate information about malaria, family planning, and maternal and child health commodities to support evidence-based decision making.

Progress during the last 12-18 months

During the past 12-18 months, PMI has been working on strengthening medicines quality monitoring (MQM) by focusing on improved laboratory management, medicines analysis, sampling and testing at the national laboratory and reinforcing the alert process when counterfeit or substandard medicines are found. Some work was disrupted due to the political situation, including implementation of MQM in Tombouctou and Kidal, but activities are currently underway in the southern part of the country.

The national laboratory still faces challenges such as limited resources and trained staff, high staff turn-over, and weak capacity in the quality assurance unit. Regulatory actions are lacking or delayed when poor quality medicines are found. Through support from PMI, the NMCP continues to participate in supervision visits and leads the quarterly malaria commodity quantification and forecasting meetings. PMI will also work with other funding organizations to help the laboratory achieve ISO accreditation, a goal that is estimated to take about two years of effort.

After suspending the program due to the political crisis, Peace Corps only recently reopened in Mali, with a small staff and a limited number of volunteers. However, there are plans to expand the program and reinstate the Malaria Volunteers in the coming year.

PMI supported the strengthening of the supply chain system and case management through continued training and supervision of staff and use of tools such as the end-use verification (EUV) and the procurement planning and monitoring report for malaria (PPMRm).

PMI also developed a dashboard to capture, track, aggregate, and disseminate information about malaria, family planning, and maternal and child health commodities to support evidence-based decision making. Training of decision makers and data managers at national, regional, and district levels started in May 2015.

Plans and justification

PMI will focus on building technical and managerial capacity at all levels of the health care system, both through implementing partners and support to the NMCP. Most inputs in training, supervision, and operational support are described elsewhere in the MOP.

Proposed activities with FY 2016 funding: ($510,000)

Strengthen the national laboratory: Provide additional training and supervision to improve the functioning and quality of the national laboratory while maintaining the current MQM program. Develop a five-year strategic plan outlining specific areas to strengthen, how to improve quality, and the sustainability of the laboratory in regards to maintaining staff, steps to take to achieve ISO 17025 accreditation, and improving the working relationship with the national regulatory authorities around counterfeit and sub-standard medicines. (*Laboratoire National de Santé)* ($100,000)

NMCP capacity building: Assist the NMCP for operations and strengthen functions. Assist NMCP's day-to-day operations and ability to work closely with PMI and implementing partners, attend supervision visits, attend conferences and trainings. Also support ensuring functionality of NMCP office per assessment conducted in FY 2014, such as providing an internet connection, computers etc. This activity will also provide some support through a PMI partner to efforts to develop a long-term sustainability strategy for the iCCM program ($200,000)

Strengthen supply chain system with better warehousing: Refurbish warehouses at the district level to meet capacity needs and proper warehousing standard for storage of malaria and other commodities. Warehouses will be chosen according to the needs, based on an existing assessment and in coordination with the Global Fund and UNDP. PMI will support improvements in warehousing for one to two warehouses that will include proper racking, climate control, equipment, and space. ($200,000)

Peace Corps: Support one Peace Corps Malaria Volunteer to assist in communication and mobilization efforts for malaria services, particularly at the community level for SMC and community case management interventions. Participate in coordination meetings to disseminate malaria action items to the PCV community. ($10,000)

Table 9: Health Systems Strengthening Activities

HSS Building Block	Technical Area	Description of Activity
Health Services	Case Management	PMI will improve, through training supervision, QA/QC systems to monitor the quality of laboratory and diagnostic services.
Health Workforce	Health Systems Strengthening	PMI will support strengthening the knowledge and capacity of the health workforce in the areas of pharmaceutical management, laboratories and diagnostics, treatment, communications and monitoring and evaluation through the various activities implemented by PMI and USAID partners. PMI will continue to support the functioning of the pharmaceutical coordination committee meetings, the MIP working group and the national RBM meetings.
Health Information	Monitoring and Evaluation	PMI will strengthen disease surveillance systems to improve decision-making, planning, forecasting and program management.
Essential Medical Products, Vaccines, and Technologies	Case Management	PMI will support improved forecasting, procurement, quality control, storage and distribution of malaria commodities, such as insecticide-treated nets, artemisinin-based combination therapies, and rapid diagnostic tests.
Health Finance	Health Systems Strengthening	PMI will assess the impact of the cost recovery system on provider practices (referenced in the OR section). PMI will also contribute to a broader effort initiated by USAID and other donors, to develop policy for the sustainability of the community health worker system. PMI's funds will go to a partner working to support this effort.
Leadership and Governance	Health Systems Strengthening	PMI will build NMCP technical and managerial capacity through training, technical assistance, and through providing supervision and support with and from implementing partners. PMI will also provide support, through the NMCP and partners, to strengthen coordination of malaria interventions, pharmaceutical regulation, development of guidelines and policies, and improve quality of services.

6. Behavior change communication

NMCP/PMI objectives

PMI supports harmonization of the national BCC strategy, ensuring consistency of messages and appropriate use of all communication channels and target audiences. An updated national BCC strategy for the period of 2014- 2018 was finalized in February 2014. The new strategy aims to support the key malaria control interventions through targeted messaging around appropriate behaviors. It has a set of core indicators focused on targeting behaviors. The strategy is divided into five communication approaches: interpersonal/counseling, community mobilization, media outlets, advocacy, and social mobilization. The various approaches will use different channels such as radio and television, brochures/pamphlets, job aids, skits/songs and "champions" to promote positive behavior change. The PMI-supported partners will coordinate their BCC activities with the NMCP and the National Center for Information, Education, and Communication for Health and will work with these partners to implement the new BCC strategy. The national BCC strategy also benefits from the support of the Global Fund, UNICEF, MSF, and other partners.

Progress since PMI was launched

Thanks to successful advocacy, there is now a malaria-specific line item in the GoM's health budget. PMI partners developed subcontracts with different radio stations and teachers' training centers, and have trained more than 7,500 youth ambassadors against malaria. A policy dialogue tool on malaria, pregnancy, and Islam, developed with PMI support, has been used with the Islamic Network for Child Survival, the Islamic Network for Population Development, and the National Union of Muslim Women. The tool is based on passages from the Koran that encourage dialogue among couples about malaria and pregnancy. Through advocacy efforts, PMI supported the development of messages on malaria-specific topics to be used by imams during Friday prayers.

In addition to the *relais*, PMI has supported the introduction of *Agents de Santé Communautaires* (Community Health Workers), a trained and paid cadre of health care workers, throughout the country. Networks of traditional healers have also been set up and supported for the detection and early referral of severe malaria cases to the health facilities. PMI BCC efforts have contributed to maintaining high ITN use among the population, increasing IPTp use from 4% in 2006 to 20% in 2012, and increasing RDT use from 47% in 2012 to 90% in 2015.

Progress during the last 12-18 months

PMI supported the finalization and dissemination of the national BCC strategy (2014-2018). Basic BCC activities occurred over the past year while waiting for the new BCC Project to launch (April 2015). During World Malaria Day, there was messaging through small plays, speeches, television, radio and booths around RDT use, SMC, seeking early treatment and correcting misinformation and myths around how one gets malaria and correct treatment. A malaria mini-series is running on television during the spring of 2015. Net use messaging is a continued part of the rolling net campaigns. The NMCP is working with partners to develop and finalize SMC messages. BCC activities have been slow to develop in Mali due to only recent strategy development and the lack of an implementing partner. Despite fairly high net coverage and use in country there is room to increase consistent net use, increase IPTp, and improve early and regular testing and treatment of malaria.

Plans and justification

PMI will disseminate the new malaria communication plan and promote related activities nationally within the larger USAID/Mali health communications project. Support and participation in World Malaria Day activities will continue. Under the new bilateral project, there will be a coordinated approach to BCC with other health interventions, but messages will be tailored to the specific issues and audiences for each intervention. The program will use various approaches to improve knowledge and attitudes around malaria, target key populations, coordinate with community leaders and stakeholders to promote healthy behaviors and support within the community. BCC activities will be closely linked with access to services activities.

Proposed activities with FY 2016 funding: ($540,000)

The following activities are intended for the integrated BCC bilateral project, but are broken out by intervention area to ensure that the project develops specifically targeted approaches for each intervention.

BCC for ITNs: Support for BCC activities will reinforce the correct use of mosquito nets throughout the year. While reported net usage is high during the high transmission season, efforts are needed to sustain usage during the low transmission season. Continuing to address the remaining barriers to correct hanging, use, and maintenance of nets and promoting year-round use is important to help meet NMCP and PMI goals. PMI will support targeted BCC messages to those who still do not use nets or are using nets seasonally, as well as encourage net repair and proper care and washing of a net. PMI will support multichannel strategies to communicate this information, including door-to-door messages disseminated by ASCs and *relais* in their communities. BCC coordination among PMI and implementing partners at the national and community levels is critical in order to ensure correct and consistent use of nets, uniformity of messages, regular monitoring, and subsequent reorientation as needed which will be implemented under the new strategic plan and under the new USAID/Mali BCC program. PMI will support BCC activities following the rolling ITN distribution campaigns to increase the use of newly distributed nets by all age groups. ($180,000)

BCC for MIP: PMI will support a multichannel strategy targeting pregnant women, women of child bearing age, and men, focusing on knowledge and perceptions related to MIP, women's awareness of risks of malaria during pregnancy, early and frequent ANC attendance at the CSCOMs, early use of IPTp in the second trimester, routine dosing with IPTp at every ANC visit, ensuring that ITNs are given free to pregnant women at their first ANC visit, and creating demand for proper treatment of MIP. These BCC activities will also include messaging for direct observation of SP administration for both health workers and pregnant women. PMI will continue to link BCC activities with other health sector messaging where appropriate. PMI will also support implementation of the new national BCC strategy, working closely with NMCP and the National Center for Information, Education, and Communication for Health, to reflect the new WHO IPTp policy recommendations. ($180,000)

BCC for case management: PMI will continue to support the dissemination of BCC messages related to case management through mass media and interpersonal communication, community mobilization and to harmonize malaria prevention and treatment messages. The strategy will promote early care-seeking for febrile children and compliance with treatment regimens. The ASCs and *relais* will also educate caregivers on signs of severe malaria that require prompt referral. PMI will support implementation of the national BCC strategy, working closely with NMCP and the National Center for Information, Education, and Communication for Health to develop and implement communication approaches and messaging on malaria case management. Strategies around SMC messaging will also be developed in line with the national communication plan. ($180,000)

7. Monitoring and evaluation

NMCP/PMI objectives

Monitoring and evaluation is a key component of Mali's national malaria strategy, and the NMCP is focused on ensuring there is a coordinated plan for malaria data capture to inform programmatic interventions and measure outcomes and impact. A national malaria M&E plan covering the years 2007-2011 was developed, costed, and adopted in 2008, and an updated M&E plan for 2013-2017 has been developed. The current plan includes routine data collection and analysis through the national health information system, or SLIS; a system for epidemic surveillance and response, a reinvigorated sentinel surveillance system; and periodic national surveys to evaluate malaria prevention and treatment activities. PMI supports the NMCP's M&E strategy through its continued support for routine system strengthening, ESR, cross-sectional surveys, and internal M&E capacity building. While the general strategy itself has not changed, with the recent political events there is an increased emphasis on improving epidemic surveillance in the northern regions of the country and improving the quality and timeliness of routine data across the country.

The NMCP's Planning and Statistical Unit oversees all M&E activities, in close collaboration with health training and research institutions. Within the NMCP, the Division of Planning and Monitoring & Evaluation is tasked with developing operational plans and monitoring and evaluating program implementation. A second NMCP unit, the Division of Epidemiological Surveillance and Research, is in charge of promoting research on malaria, establishing an early warning system to detect and respond to malaria epidemics, and supporting operational units in epidemic response.

Progress since PMI was launched

Routine System Strengthening: Mali's M&E system relies on malaria data collected routinely through the SLIS, but the quality of these data is variable and feedback is not delivered in a timely manner to assist program planning and management. SLIS data are compiled every three months and reported annually. These data theoretically include both confirmed and unconfirmed cases, but diagnostics were not systematically implemented until recent years. The 2014 data from the SLIS, shows that, on average, 90% of suspected malaria cases are tested in Mali, and 76% are confirmed to be malaria. The NMCP hopes to increase the health system's capacity to collect, analyze, report, and use these data for programmatic decision-making.

PMI has supported enhancements to the malaria portion of the routine information system for several years to increase the timeliness and quality of the malaria component of the SLIS. These enhancements included revisions to the reporting forms for the malaria sections, conducting training and supervisory activities, improving the technology infrastructure, and implementing an SMS reporting system in selected districts. In FY 2013 and FY 2014, the system was expanded to two new regions, and a mobile data transmission system (using SMS) was implemented in selected districts. The system allows the NMCP to have access, via a website, to monthly data on epidemiologic indicators for each of the implementation districts. In FY 2015, the system will be expanded to PMI IRS and SMC sites. PMI has also supported NMCP staff to participate in regional workshops on the monitoring and evaluation of malaria programs.

Household Surveys: Population-based surveys currently provide the most accurate data on malaria intervention coverage and malaria biomarkers (i.e., anemia and parasitemia). Following a DHS in 2006, a national anemia and parasitemia (A&P) survey conducted with PMI support in 2010 during the peak transmission period (September-October) provided the first parasitemia measures in Mali (see below for national estimates of anemia and parasitemia). A DHS including parasitemia biomarkers was conducted in 2012, and a health facility survey, which provided data on the quality of malaria case management and antenatal care, was also conducted in the high transmission season in 2012. The 2012-2013 DHS showed greatly increased levels of coverage for key interventions, and a corresponding decline in child mortality rates (data shown in Strategy section, under *Progress on coverage/impact indicators to date*). However, the survey results for biomarkers of malaria and anemia continued to be high as well. Results reflect high transmission season estimates and showed that 52% of children 6-59 months of age were parasitemic by microscopy and 21% had severe anemia (hemoglobin <7g/dL). These results are concerning and the NMCP and partners are focused on reducing these levels in the coming years. An MIS is planned in FY 2015 to track progress towards these goals.

Progress during the last 12-18 months

PMI had continued to support the expansion of the enhanced routine reporting system started in 2011. This activity has included the establishment of a national steering committee to guide the development and roll out of the project. In each district targeted for enhancement, the site is equipped with necessary technology (computer, SMS, or paper-based) and the district and health facility teams are trained on data quality, reporting, and information use. District teams are also trained on M&E supervisory procedures. To date, 18 of the 60 health districts in Mali are covered, representing 18 CSREFs and 381 CSCOMs. Of the CSCOMs, 63 are using the pilot SMS data transmission system. Using FY 2015 funds, the system is expanding to two additional districts focused on PMI's IRS and SMC sites (two districts for IRS and ten districts for SMC). A quality assessment of this enhanced reporting system conducted in 2014 showed that 95% of targeted facilities reported each month, and facilities using tally sheets decreased their compilation time from 15 hours to 4 hours per month. PMI also provides support to the NMCP for quarterly malaria data reviews and reporting. In addition, the USAID Mission and other donors are investing in the development of a DHIS2 system for the HMIS, addressing needs that were identified in a large national assessment in 2015. As this activity develops, PMI and its partners are working with the DHIS2 implementers to ensure that the malaria indicators are fully captured in the new system and that the SMS data transfer is compatible with the DHIS2 system.

PMI also supported the development of an epidemic and response system for the Mopti Region, designed to provide timely data regarding outbreaks in the region with the highest parasitemia and the largest number of people displaced from the North. At the start of 2015, the system was operational in three pilot districts, with plans to complete coverage of the Mopti Region by the end of the year. To date, 25 data managers in the Mopti Region were trained in outbreak detection and reporting procedures, and the pilot CSCOMs have been equipped with computers and internet capacity to record and transmit data. Taken together, the improved routine reporting and the epidemic surveillance system provide timely and accurate epidemiologic data to the NMCP for better program management and outbreak response.

The table below shows the main sources of data and sequence of surveys for malaria program monitoring and impact evaluations.

Table 10. Data Sources for Monitoring and Evaluation in Mali, 2010 – 2018

Data Source	Survey Activities	Calendar Year								
		2010	2011	2012	2013	2014	2015	2016	2017	2018
National-level Household surveys	Demographic Health Survey (DHS)			X						X
	Malaria Indicator Survey (MIS)							X		
	MICS survey	X								
	A&P survey	X								
Health Facility and Other Surveys	Health facility survey				X				X	
	EUV survey			X	X	X	X	X	X	X
Malaria Surveillance and Routine System Support	Support to Epidemic Surveillance in Northern Mali					X	X	X	X	X
	Support to parallel routine malaria info system (for GF or other reporting)	X	X	X	X	X	X	X	X	X
	Support to HMIS							X	X	X
Therapeutic Efficacy monitoring	In vivo efficacy testing for first/second-line drugs						X		X	
	SP Efficacy monitoring								X	
Entomology	Entomological surveillance and resistance monitoring	X	X	X	X	X	X	X	X	X
Other malaria-related evaluations	RTI IRS Coverage Survey/ Barriers to IPTp Study		X							
	Culture of Net Use Study				X					
Other Data Sources	Malaria Impact Evaluation						X			

Plans and justification

Following democratic elections in Mali, the PMI program has rapidly regained ground that was lost during the crisis. Monitoring and evaluation activities play an integral role in responding to established PMI needs for program monitoring and impact assessment. The major focus of M&E activities in 2016 will be the continuation of the enhanced routine information system in existing sites and an expansion to two additional regions. The expansion of the enhanced malaria information system will provide timely and accurate data for the NMCP to monitor trends in epidemiologic indicators. The routine system strengthening activity will also expand the use of SMS for more timely and accurate reporting of data. In addition, PMI will support activities to integrate the malaria indicators and reporting into the nascent DHIS2 system as it develops. The ultimate goal is to integrate entirely with DHIS2 but the timeline for that will depend on the speed of the DHIS2 rollout. The implementing partner for this activity changed in 2015, and a new HMIS project was awarded, thus slightly delaying the full planning of the activity. In FY 2016, a full timetable for the roll out of HMIS support activities will be developed. This activity will also include support to the NMCP for an annual report on malaria data.

The last health facility survey in Mali was conducted in 2013. In the interim, Mali has made much progress on improving the quality of care for case management, including addressing numerous supply chain issues, improving diagnostic quality assurance, and training health facility and community-based providers on malaria diagnosis and treatment. In addition, Mali has changed its MIP protocols to reflect the revised WHO recommendations and invested considerably in rolling out these new policies through training and supervision. Using FY 2016 funds, PMI plans to support a health facility survey to monitor the quality of care of routine case management and MIP services at the CSCOM level, identify barriers and challenges and propose adequate solutions for findings. Other USAID health elements (Maternal and Child Health (MCH), Family Planning and Reproductive Health (FP/RH) and Nutrition/WASH are interested and will co-fund the survey. Co-funding will be also sought from other donor organizations to ensure a more comprehensive survey that captures broader health data beyond malaria.

With SP now being used nationally for IPTp and for SMC in more than 50% of the country, WHO recommends including vigilant resistance monitoring in targeted sites. Mali has not routinely conducted resistance monitoring for SP previously and there are concerns that such widespread use of the drug through two different interventions might create pressure for resistance. PMI will support resistance monitoring in four sites with significant overlap of IPTp and SMC programming.

WHO and PMI recommend therapeutic efficacy testing every 2-3 years. In Mali, PMI supported TES in 2015 for both AL and ASAQ, the first and second-line antimalarials used in the country. This project is done in collaboration the Laboratory of Applied Molecular Biology of the University of Bamako. Funding for one site is provided through a grant from NIH, and PMI supports two additional sites. Additional details are available in the Case Management section. In addition to routine TES, the sites provide molecular samples for global surveillance of K13 mutations.

In 2018, Mali is planning a DHS survey. With FY 2016 funds, PMI will support the initial planning and survey design activities to ensure that malaria indicators and issues are incorporated into the larger survey effort.

Proposed activities with FY 2016 funding: ($1,460,000)

Routine system strengthening: PMI supports improvements in the M&E system at the CSCOM and CSREF levels in Mali to improve malaria data quality and use. In FY 2016, PMI intends to build on accomplishments in improved routine reporting from health facilities by continuing to support the existing sites, and expanding the revised system to SMC and IRS districts. This activity will support training and quality control/timeliness for completion of routine SLIS reporting forms, assist in analysis and feedback on malaria indicators and promote use of findings at all levels to improve program performance. This activity will continue to support the mobile data transfer system (SMS) in USAID-targeted regions to facilitate timely malaria surveillance. This activity will also support efforts to include malaria data in the DHIS2 system as it develops. ($500,000)

Support for 2017 Health Facility Survey: Support for a nationally representative health facility survey to monitor progress in quality of care for routine case management and malaria in pregnancy interventions. Co-funding from other USAID health elements and other donors will be sought to complement PMI funding. ($250,000)

Resistance monitoring for SP: Support for SP resistance monitoring in four sites. ($100,000)

Therapeutic Efficacy Surveillance (TES): TES of first and second-line antimalarials in two sites. ($100,000)

DHS Survey: Mali plans a DHS in 2018. This funding will enable the initial planning and survey design activities to begin in 2017. ($500,000)

CDC TDY: Technical assistance to provide support for monitoring and evaluation activities. ($10,000)

8. Operational research

The NMCP and PMI share a common goal of conducting operational research to answer specific questions regarding the implementation and effectiveness of critical interventions. The OR studies proposed for support by PMI are identified jointly and designed to respond to key information needs in the NMCP's National Strategic Plan.

Progress since PMI was launched

Since the launch of PMI in Mali in 2008, multiple studies have been conducted in Mali that have helped inform malaria control and prevention activities. In October 2008, a mixed-method evaluation was conducted to: (1) evaluate the validity of the expanded programme on immunization (EPI) contact method as a tool for monitoring bednet usage and treatment of common childhood illnesses by comparing data collected using the EPI contact method to that collected during baseline and follow-up representative cross-sectional household surveys; and (2) evaluate the effectiveness of the EPI contact method as an intervention to improve bednet use and the appropriate treatment of common childhood illnesses. One intervention district (EPI-contact method) and one comparison district were selected in the Segou Region, and both qualitative (key informant interviews, exit interviews, and focus groups) and quantitative methods (baseline and follow-up surveys) were used. The primary outcome measures were determinants of ITN use and appropriate treatment of fever in children. Results showed that the EPI contact method did not produce consistent measures of ITN utilization on a monthly basis. Health workers felt the EPI contact method lengthened the waiting time for vaccination. Observations and focus groups identified poor ITN durability as a concern and mothers' impressions that ITNs last approximately 6 months[4]. Results of the validity comparison of the EPI contact method and household survey data showed that the EPI contact method did not produce reliable estimates of health behaviors[5].

From 2009 to 2010, a study was conducted to develop a dry season malaria vector control strategy in the Sudan savannah areas of Mali. A pretest/post-test design was implemented to assess the impact of the IRS performed in eight Niger River bank hamlets on malaria transmission parameters of two larger villages located at 2-3 kilometers from the river. Monthly entomological monitoring through the rainy season was conducted following the IRS campaign to measure entomological indicators of malaria transmission. Results from 2009 showed some reductions in *Anopheles* densities per house in two of the three IRS river hamlets (Dangassa-Somonosso and Bozokin) but little difference in a third (Fourda). Similarly, *Anopheles* biting rates were reduced in Dangassa-Somonosso but not in the other two IRS river hamlets. No reductions in *Anopheles* densities or biting rates were seen in inland villages. Results in 2010 were more positive but also mixed. The IRS-treated hamlets showed significant reductions in resting densities, biting rates, and EIRs during the first three months; clearly demonstrating the effectiveness of IRS. After three months however, mosquito densities, biting rates, and EIRs quickly returned to pre-intervention levels. Cone assays performed on sprayed walls showed that ICON 10 CS (lambda-cyhalothrin) lasted only 3-4 months before activity fell well below 80% mortality thresholds; the different microclimates and interior household characteristics may explain results that diverge from the IRS districts where lambda-cyhalothrin remained active for 6 - 8 months. In addition, resistance to pyrethroids was detected at high levels in the study area

----

[4] Wei SC, Vanden Eng JL, Patterson AE, *et. al.* 2012. Effect of the expanded program on immunization contact method of data collection on health behaviors in Mali. JID, 205: S103-11.
[5] Wei SC, Vanden Eng JL, Patterson AE, *et. al.* 2012. Validity of expanded program on immunization contact method health behavior estimates in Mali. JID, 205: S112-19.

(only 50 and 56% mortality in WHO assays for permethrin and lambda-cyhalothrin, respectively).

Another vector control intervention was conducted in 2009 to determine the added benefit of larviciding water sources surrounding houses that received IRS compared to houses that received only IRS. Larval control, mosquito densities, sporozoite rates, and entomological inoculation rates were assessed before and after the intervention in 2-3 villages in each arm (IRS only and IRS+larviciding) in 2009 and 2010. In both years, there was a highly significant reduction in larval breeding activity in the villages with larviciding compared to IRS only villages; in 2009 entomological measurements varied widely by location so overall there was no difference seen between intervention arms; however, in 2010 significant differences were seen in resting densities, biting rates, sporozoite rates, and EIRs between intervention arms. Investigators concluded that some benefit was seen with larviciding combined with IRS compared to IRS alone.

A USAID centrally-funded study was conducted to estimate the financial implications of removing malaria user fees (consultation, laboratory diagnosis, drugs) for children under five in primary care level/private nonprofit facilities (CSCOM) and first level public facilities (CSREF) in Mali and on third party payers. Facility and patient exit surveys, in-depth interviews, and a costing model were conducted in 40 health facilities. There was consensus among providers and stakeholders that the removal of fees was important to increase access to care, especially among the poor and the majority rural population, and decrease infant mortality. However, several concerns/challenges included potential substantial financial losses to facilities, increase in demand for services and abusive increase in utilization, which risk overcrowding health facilities, decreased quality of care, and the absence of a coherent framework that identifies real costs and proper financing mechanisms and sources. There were also strong practical objections to the removal of only malaria user fees such as being a non-feasible option, and a desire to remove all under-five user fees. According to the costing model, total estimated losses to primary care and first level reference health facilities in Mali ranged between cfa 0.34 billion and cfa 0.45 billion (approximately $0.72 million and $0.95 million), depending on utilization changes. Total estimated costs to a third party range between cfa 1.1 billion and cfa 1.6 billion (approximately $2.33 million and $3.4 million). The higher figures equal 2.4% of the Ministry of Health's 2009 approved budget.

Progress during the last 12-18 months

During the last 12-18 months, two OR studies have made significant progress:

Combination ITNs: The field study comparing new 'combination' ITN products on entomological measures of malaria transmission and ITN integrity began in June 2013 when, vector populations from candidate study villages were screened to confirm the presence of elevated mixed function oxidases (the resistance mechanism targeted by the 'combination' nets).

Starting October 2013, monthly vector collections were conducted to establish baselines. ITNs were distributed in February–March of 2014, and data collection is ongoing.

SMC: The baseline survey to measure prevalence of anemia and parasitemia in children ages 3-59 months in the intervention (SMC) and comparison districts was conducted July 23 – August 2, 2014. Prevalence of fever and parasitemia were similar in intervention (23.4%) and control (29.5%) districts prior to SMC (p=0.34). After SMC, parasitemia prevalence fell to 18% in the intervention district and increased to 46% in the control district (Difference-in-differences (DD) OR=0.35; 95% CI: 0.20-0.60). SMC also significantly reduced the odds of malaria disease (DD OR=0.20; 95% CI: 0.04-0.94) and moderate anemia (Hb<8 g/dL) (DD OR=0.26, 95% CI: 0.11-0.65). Rounds 1 – 4 of SMC adherence surveys were completed in November 2014. Preliminary results showed that the proportion of children who received SMC drugs at least on day one, dropped from 82% in Round 1 to 68% in Round 4. The proportion of children who received SMC drugs on days two and three at home remained high (>90%) between rounds one to four.

Table 11. PMI-funded Operational Research Studies

Completed OR Studies			
Title	**Start date**	**End date**	**Budget**
A mixed-methods evaluation of the expanded program on immunization contact method as both a monitoring tool and intervention for malaria control and prevention in Mali.	10/2008	10/2009	$185,000
Development of a pilot dry season vector control strategy in Mali.	06/2009	06/2010	$80,000
Integrated vector management: Interaction of larval control and IRS on *Anopheles gambiae* density and vectorial capacity for human malaria.	06/2009	12/2010	$110,000
The financial implications of removing user fees for malaria treatment for under-five children in Mali.	09/2010	06/2011	
Ongoing OR Studies			
Title	**Start date**	**End date**	**Budget**
A field study comparing the impact of new 'combination' long-lasting insecticidal (mosquito) net products on entomological measures of malaria transmission: Olyset Plus® and PermaNet 3.0® versus their conventional ITN analogues: Olyset® and PermaNet 2.0®.	06/2013	12/2016	$433,000
Evaluation of seasonal malaria chemoprevention (SMC) pilot in Kita District, Mali.	07/2014	04/2016	$314,000
Planned OR Studies FY 2016			
Title	**Start date (est.)**	**End date (est.)**	**Budget**
Economics of health provider behavior in the Bamako Initiative environment.			$200,000
Increasing IPTp uptake through enhanced antenatal clinic service delivery to improve maternal and child health.			$100,000

Plans and justification

The Bamako Initiative aimed to increase access to primary health care by raising the effectiveness, efficiency, financial viability, and equity of health services. Bamako Initiative health centers implement an integrated minimum health-care package in order to meet basic community health needs, focusing on access to drugs and regular contact between health-care providers and communities. Numerous systematic reviews have been conducted to assess the quality of impact of user fees on health service utilization, household expenditures and health outcomes in low- and middle- income countries. However, there have not been any evidence-based studies to evaluate the concern that the need to generate revenue in a cost recovery system affects health care provider behavior. Anecdotal evidence suggests that providers might be conducting additional tests or prescribing unnecessary medications in order to generate funds.

The objective of this study is to compare and evaluate diagnostic and prescribing practices of health care workers within the context of cost recovery. The specifics of the OR study will be developed jointly with the OR committee and the Malian research community.

Despite ongoing PMI support of malaria in pregnancy activities, IPTp uptake has been low. Utilization of ANC services is moderate, but the 2012-2013 DHS reported the proportion of women who received two or more doses of IPTp during their last pregnancy at 20%, well below the PMI targets for IPTp. The NMCP is committed to the new WHO policy on providing pregnant women with a minimum of three doses of IPTp. Preparedness for national level implementation is underway, however in order to effectively implement this new policy the barriers identified in empirical studies in the country must be addressed. These multi-faceted barriers suggest a significant missed opportunity to deliver effective ANC services and IPTp. Given the logistical, practical, and financial challenges together with the context of Mali just emerging from a profound socio-political crisis, sound evidence is needed to provide the best opportunity of successful implementation of the new IPTp policy. Specifically, PMI will test an enhanced intervention package which combines intensive training (including simulated ANC consultations) and job aids, with regular and specific supervision to improve provider behaviors around IPTp dispensing. This enhanced package will be tested on its own, and with a program of community mobilization, and compared against districts receiving routine ANC activities. Reprogrammed FY 2015 and FY 2016 funds will be requested to support two years of data collection, data analysis, and report writing for this MIP OR study.

Proposed activities with FY 2016 funding: ($300,000)

Evaluation of the impact of cost recovery systems on health provider behavior: PMI plans to support an OR study to evaluate the possible implications of a cost recovery system on diagnostic and prescription practices for malaria. In Mali, basic malaria diagnosis and treatment are supposed to be free for children under five years of age. In the past, malaria constituted a very basic source of income for primary health care facilities as it was, and continues to be a major cause of disease among Malian children. With the advent of PMI, diagnosis and treatment were made free, thus removing a primary source of revenue. There are anecdotal concerns that this phenomenon might affect provider practices in terms of preferences for types of diagnostic tests or drugs provided. This study aims to evaluate this phenomenon and determine whether this is a concern in Mali and, if so, provide basic information around which remedial strategies and policies can be developed. ($200,000)

Evaluation of an enhanced intervention package to improve uptake of IPTp: PMI will support year two of this research study to assess the coverage of at least three doses of IPTp achieved with standard or enhanced intervention packages. ($100,000)

9. Staffing and administration

Two health professionals serve as resident advisors to oversee PMI in Mali, one representing CDC and one representing USAID. In addition, one or more Foreign Service Nationals (FSNs) work as part of the PMI team. All PMI staff members are part of a single interagency team led by the USAID Mission Director or his/her designee in country. The PMI team shares responsibility for development and implementation of PMI strategies and work plans, coordination with national authorities, managing collaborating agencies and supervising day-to-day activities. Candidates for resident advisor positions (whether initial hires or replacements) will be evaluated and/or interviewed jointly by USAID and CDC, and both agencies will be involved in hiring decisions, with the final decision made by the individual agency.

The PMI professional staff work together to oversee all technical and administrative aspects of PMI, including finalizing details of the project design, implementing malaria prevention and treatment activities, monitoring and evaluation of outcomes and impact, reporting of results, and providing guidance to PMI partners.

The PMI lead in country is the USAID Mission Director. The day-to-day lead for PMI is delegated to the USAID Health Office Director and thus the two PMI resident advisors, one from USAID and one from CDC, report to the USAID Health Office Director for day-to-day leadership, and work together as a part of a single interagency team. The technical expertise housed in Atlanta and Washington guides PMI programmatic efforts.

The two PMI resident advisors are based within the USAID health office and are expected to spend approximately half their time sitting with and providing technical assistance to the national malaria control programs and partners.

Locally-hired staff to support PMI activities either in Ministries or in USAID will be approved by the USAID Mission Director. Because of the need to adhere to specific country policies and USAID accounting regulations, any transfer of PMI funds directly to Ministries or host governments will need to be approved by the USAID Mission Director and Controller, in addition to the US Global Malaria Coordinator.

Proposed activities with FY 2016 funding: ($1,252,917)

CDC technical and administrative support ($350,000)
USAID technical and administrative support ($902,917)

Table 1: Budget Breakdown by Mechanism

President's Malaria Initiative – Mali

Planned Malaria Obligations for FY 2016

Mechanism	Geographic Area	Activity	Budget ($)	%
TBD-Supply Chain Contract	National	Procurement, distribution of malaria commodities and supply chain strengthening	11,901,000	48%
Abt IRS T06	2 districts and 13 sites	Procure insecticide equipment, technical assistance to implement spraying and entomological monitoring	4,697,083	19%
CDC IAA	National	Salary and support for CDC RA, technical assistance from CDC staff	409,000	2%
GEMS	IRS areas	Environmental monitoring	40,000	<1%
SSGI	4 Regions (Koulikoro, Sikasso, Bamako, Kayes, Gao when security allows)	Training on case management and supervision of all aspects of case management. Specific to USAID focus provinces	3,160,000	13%
KJK Project (BCC Bilateral)	National	Conduct BCC activities for ITN, IRS, Case Management, MIP	540,000	2%
TBD-M&E	National	Health Facility survey	250,000	1%
MalariaCare	National (focus on Mopti and Segou)	Training on case management and supervision of all aspects of case management. Specific to non-USAID focus provinces	500,000	2%
TBD-OR	National (focus on Mopti and Segou)	Implementation of OR study on enhanced package of MIP to improve IPTp	100,000	<1%
PQM	National	Strengthen quality assurance and quality	500,000	2%

		control of antimalarials.		
Health Finance and Governance	National	Support day-to-day operations of the NMCP, and fund study on economics and health provider behavior in a cost recovery system environment	400,000	2%
TBD - Pharmaceutical management	National	Strengthen pharmaceutical management and the supply chain system at national, district and community levels. Emphasis on improving quantification, forecasting and distribution	600,000	2%
Measure Evaluation	National	Routine monitoring system strengthening	500,000	2%
DHS Program	National	Planning for 2018 DHS	500,000	2%
USAID	National	Staffing and Admin	902,917	4%
Total			**25,000,000**	**100%**

Table 2: Budget Breakdown by Activity

President's Malaria Initiative – Mali

Planned Malaria Obligations for FY 2016

Proposed Activity	Mechanism	Budget		Geographic Area	Description
		Total $	Commodity $		
PREVENTIVE ACTIVITIES					
Insecticide-treated Nets					
Procurement of ITNs	TBD-Supply Chain Contract	6,002,000	6,002,000	Nationwide	PMI will procure 1,500,000 ITNs to support the routine distribution to children under one year of age and pregnant women through routine services nationwide. It is anticipated that the needs for mass campaign to replace nets distributed in 2014 and prior will be covered by the Global Fund.
Distribution of ITNs	TBD-Supply Chain Contract	123,000	0	Nationwide	PMI will support the distribution of 1.5 million free ITNs through routine ANC and immunization services at the CSCOM level for infants and pregnant women. PMI will also support steps to ensure that ITNs reach the targeted populations (ensure that health workers are distributing ITNs according to national guidance, verifying stocks, and comparing data for nets distributed versus physical stock).These funds are PMI's contribution to the overall distribution system which is also supported by other donors and the GoM.
Subtotal ITNs		**6,125,000**	**6,002,000**		
Indoor Residual Spraying					

Activity	Description	Location			Mechanism
Indoor residual spraying	Procure IRS equipment (insecticide, sprayers, etc.), training, implementation, data collection, protocols, guidelines, BCC, logistic assessment, technical assistance for spraying/entomological assessment (CDC IAA).	2 districts Koulikoro and Baroueli	1,560,000	4,397,081	Abt IRS2 T06
Entomological monitoring	Conduct annual entomological monitoring. Support the NMCP entomologist in conducting IRS-related entomological monitoring. Strengthen capacity of DHPS to participate in the monitoring of IRS operations, training of spray operators and to provide coordination with NMCP on district IRS operations. Mapping insecticide resistance and mosquito biting behavior nationwide.	13 sites	0	300,000	Abt IRS2 T06
Procurement of supplies for entomological monitoring	Procure and transport specialized entomological equipment from CDC/Atlanta to Mali for entomological monitoring activities		0	10,000	CDC IAA
Environmental compliance monitoring	Conduct environmental compliance monitoring in 2 IRS districts according to PMI guidance.	2 districts Koulikoro and Baroueli	0	40,000	GEMS
Technical Assistance	Technical assistance from CDC entomologist for monitoring IRS implementation		0	29,000	CDC IAA
Subtotal IRS			**1,560,000**	**4,776,0831**	
Malaria in Pregnancy					
Procurement of SP	Procure 2 million SP doses to cover the annual need for the estimated 700,000 pregnant women attending ANC in 2017, including handling and distribution costs.	Nationwide	300,000	300,000	TBD-Supply Chain Contract
Strengthen FANC and MIP services	Continue to work with the NMCP and partners to improve the FANC and MIP services, including the roll out of the updated MIP guidelines, support training of health providers, and ensure provision of free SP for IPTp. Work with the MoH Reproductive Health Division and the	4 Regions (Koulikoro, Sikasso, Bamako, Kayes, Gao when security allows)	0	450,000	SSGI

72

Activity	Mechanism			Location	Description
					Midwives Association, to expand use of the in-service FANC training module and increase supportive supervision during IPTp implementation nationally through facility and community outreach activities
Subtotal Malaria in Pregnancy		750,000	300,000		
SUBTOTAL PREVENTIVE		11,651,083	7,862,000		
CASE MANAGEMENT					
Diagnosis and Treatment					
Procurement of RDTs	TBD-Supply Chain Contract	1,550,000	1,550,000	Nationwide	Procure 3,000,000 RDTs
Procurement of ACTs	TBD-Supply Chain Contract	1,360,000	1,360,000	Nationwide	Procure 500,000 treatments of ACTs for public sector and 360,000 treatments during SMC campaign in all 40 districts.
Procurement of injectable artesunate for treatment of severe malaria	TBD-Supply Chain Contract	420,000	420,000	Nationwide	Procure 96,000 treatments of injectable artesunate for treatment of patients with severe malaria at CSREF (and selected CSCOM) levels. Also procure syringes and gloves.
Distribution of ACTs, RDTs, SP and other malaria commodities to the district level	TBD-Supply Chain Contract	250,000	-	Nationwide	Distribution of malaria commodities (ACTs, RDTS, SP, severe malaria meds to the district level

Activity	Partner			Location	Description
Training and supervision for case management	SSGI	600,000	0	4 USAID focus regions (Koulikoro, Sikasso, Bamako, Kayes)	Training includes diagnostics, case management for simple and severe malaria, and supervision on all aspects of case management. SSGI will cover the four USAID focus regions for this intervention.
Training and supervision for case management	MalariaCare	500,000	0	Mopti and Segou Regions	Training includes diagnostics, case management for simple and severe malaria, and supervision on all aspects of case management in Mopti and Segou Regions which are not covered under the four USAID Regions.
Procurement of medications for SMC	TBD-Supply Chain Contract	1,696,000	1,696,000	10 Districts in the 4 USAID focus regions (Koulikoro, Sikasso, Bamako, Kayes)	Cover approximately 800,000 children < 5 years with four rounds of SP-AQ co-blister for SMC. Assumes cost of $0.53 per treatment per child (x 4 rounds).
Implementation of SMC (training, supervision, distribution)	SSGI	1,500,000	0	10 Districts in the 4 USAID focus regions	Implement SMC in USAID focus regions. Implementation will include the costs of training, supervision, community mobilization, and distribution of drugs
Implementation of iCCM	SSGI	600,000	0	4 USAID focus regions (Koulikoro, Sikasso, Bamako, Kayes)	Implementation of iCCM in the four USAID focus regions. Support for iCCM includes support to the malaria/fever component of the iCCM package, with new and refresher trainings at district levels, supportive supervision, training, monitoring and evaluation, and provision of ASC materials and supplies. PMI will continue to support the NMCP to coordinate all community health implementing partner activities.
CDC TDY for diagnostics	CDC IAA	10,000	0		Provide technical assistance for the quality assurance of diagnostics
Subtotal Diagnosis and Treatment		**8,486,000**	**5,026,000**		

Pharmaceutical Management

Supply chain and logistics strengthening	TBD	Strengthen pharmaceutical management and the supply chain system at national, district and community levels. Emphasis on improving, quantification, forecasting and distribution.	Nationwide	0	500,000
End-use verification	TBD	Conduct at least two end-use verification surveys, tracking commodities down to community level and case management practices with an emphasis on follow-up of findings.	Nationwide	0	100,000
Strengthen quality assurance and quality control of antimalarials	PQM	Strengthen capacity in quality assurance and quality control of antimalarials via increased training at the national laboratory, supporting the implementation of the five year strategic plan, supervision of MQM sites and improving the alert system around counterfeit and substandard medicines.	Nationwide	0	200,000
Subtotal Pharmaceutical Management				0	**800,000**
SUBTOTAL CASE MANAGEMENT				**5,026,000**	**9,286,000**
HEALTH SYSTEM STRENGTHENING / CAPACITY BUILDING					
Strengthen national laboratory capacity (LNS)	PQM	Provide additional training and supervision to improve the functioning and quality of national laboratory while maintaining the current MQM program. Develop a five year strategic plan outlining specific areas to strengthen, how to improve quality and the sustainability of the lab in regards to maintaining staff, steps to take to achieve ISO 17025 accreditation and improving the regulatory and alert systems around counterfeit and sub-standard medicines.		0	100,000

Activity	Partner	Amount		Location	Description
Support day to day operations of NMCP	Health Finance and Governance	200,000	0	National level	Assist the NMCP for operations and strengthen functions. Assist NMCP's day-to-day operations and ability to work closely with PMI and implementing partners, attend supervision visits, attend conferences and trainings. Also support ensuring functionality of NMCP office per assessment conducted in FY14, such as providing an internet connection, computers etc. These funds will also be used by the partner to support national efforts to develop a long-term strategy for sustainability of the iCCM program.
Refurbishment of warehouses at district level	TBD-Supply Chain Contract	200,000	0	District level	Refurbish warehouses at the district level to meet capacity needs and proper warehousing standard for storage of malaria and other commodities. Warehouses will be chosen according to the needs, based on an existing assessment and in coordination with the Global Fund and UNDP.
Support in areas of communication and mobilization of malaria activities	SSGI (Peace Corps)	10,000	0	Sikasso Region	Support for one Peace Corps Malaria Volunteer in Sikasso Region to support communication, mobilization and improve data collection for malaria activities.
SUBTOTAL HSS & CAPACITY BUILDING		**510,000**	**0**		
BEHAVIOR CHANGE COMMUNICATION					
BCC for ITNs	KJK Project (BCC bilateral)	180,000	0	Nationwide	Support for BCC activities to reinforce the correct hanging, use, and maintenance of mosquito nets. Support multichannel strategies for communicate and BCC coordination among PMI and implementing partners at the national and community levels. PMI will also support BCC activities following the rolling ITN distribution campaigns.
BCC for MIP interventions	KJK Project (BCC bilateral)	180,000	0	Nationwide	Support a multichannel strategy targeting pregnant women, women of child bearing age, and men, focusing on knowledge and perceptions related to MIP, women's awareness of risks of malaria during pregnancy, early and frequent ANC attendance at the CSCOMs, early and regular use of IPTp, ITN distribution and use. PMI will also support

implementation of the new national BCC strategy.

Activity	Description	Location		Amount	Implementer
BCC for Case Management	Support the dissemination of BCC messages related to case management through mass media and interpersonal communication, community mobilization and to harmonize malaria prevention and treatment messages. The strategy will promote early care-seeking for febrile children and compliance with treatment regimens. PMI will support implementation of the national BCC strategy, working closely with NMCP and the National Center for Information, Education, and Communication for Health to develop and implement communication approaches and messaging on malaria case management.	Nationwide	0	180,000	KJK Project (BCC bilateral)
SUBTOTAL BCC			0	**540,000**	
MONITORING AND EVALUATION					
Routine system strengthening	Extend improved routine reporting from health facilities by continuing to support the existing sites, and expanding the revised system to SMC and IRS districts. This activity will support training and quality control/timeliness for completion of routine SLIS reporting forms, assist in analysis and feedback on malaria indicators and promote use of findings at all levels to improve program performance. This activity will continue to support the mobile data transfer system (SMS) in USAID-targeted regions to facilitate timely malaria surveillance.	Nationwide	0	500,000	Measure Evaluation
Health Facility Survey	Nationwide health facility survey to monitoring provider behaviors and adherence to new case management and MIP policies.	Nationwide	0	250,000	TBD
SP resistance monitoring for SMC sites	Resistance monitoring for SP in the context of SMC expansion as per WHO recommendations. MRTC is the recognized appropriate laboratory for this work in Mali.	4 sites	0	100,000	USP/PQM (to MRTC)

TES	USP/PQM (LBMA)	100,000	0	2 sites	Routine monitoring of therapeutic efficacy of first and second-line drugs
DHS	DHS Program	500,000	0	0	Planning for 2018 DHS
CDC M&E TDY	CDC IAA	10,000	0	0	Technical assistance from CDC M&E specialist
SUBTOTAL M&E		**1,460,000**	**0**		
OPERATIONS RESEARCH					
Evaluation of impact of cost recovery systems on health care provider behavior	Health Finance and Governance	200,000	0	4 USAID focus regions (Koulikoro, Sikasso, Bamako, Kayes)	Evaluation of the impact of cost recovery systems at the health facility level on health care provider diagnostic and treatment practices.
MIP Study	TBD	100,000	0	Segou	Evaluation of a pilot of enhanced MIP service delivery on uptake of IPTp.
SUBTOTAL OR		**300,000**	**0**		
IN-COUNTRY STAFFING AND ADMINISTRATION					
CDC	CDC	350,000	0	Nationwide	Support for CDC PMI Resident Advisor (1) with salary and benefits
USAID	USAID	902,917	0	Nationwide	Support for USAID PMI staff (1 PSC/1 FSN) with salaries, benefits, contribution to salaries and benefits of Mission support staff, IT support costs, office space, vehicles, other Mission program support costs, local costs for CDC PMI Advisor.
SUBTOTAL IN-COUNTRY STAFFING		**1,252,917**	**0**		
GRAND TOTAL		**25,000,000**	**12,888,000**